DREAMING WHILE AWAKE

Other books by Arnold Mindell

Quantum Mind: The Edge between Physics and Psychology

Sitting in the Fire: Large Group Transformation Using Conflict and Diversity

The Shaman's Body: A New Shamanism for Transforming Health, Relationships, and Community

The Leader as Martial Artist: An Introduction to Deep Democracy

The Year I: Global Process Work with Planetary Tensions

Inner Dreambodywork: Working on Yourself Alone

Riding the Horse Backwards: Process Work in Theory and Practice

Coma, Key to Awakening: Working with the Dreambody near Death

City Shadows: Psychological Interventions in Psychiatry

The Dreambody in Relationships

River's Way, The Process Science of the Dreambody

Working with the Dreaming Body

Dreambody: The Body's Role in Revealing the Self

DREAMING WHILE AWAKE

techniques for 24-hour lucid dreaming

ARNOLD MINDELL Ph.D.

HAMPTON ROADS
PUBLISHING COMPANY, INC.

for the evolving human spirit

Cover design by Grace Pedalino
Cover photo © PhotoDisc
Interior art by Rebecca Whitney

For information write:

Hampton Roads Publishing Company, Inc.
1125 Stoney Ridge Road
Charlottesville, VA 22902

Or call: 804-296-2772
FAX: 804-296-5096
e-mail: hrpc@hrpub.com
Web site: www.hrpub.com

If you are unable to order this book from your local
bookseller, you may order directly from the publisher.
Quantity discounts for organizations are available.
Call 1-800-766-8009, toll-free.

Library of Congress Catalog Card Number: 99-68253

ISBN 1-57174-187-9

10 9 8 7 6 5 4 3 2 1

Printed on acid-free paper in the United States

Dreaming is the Mystical Source of Reality

Contents

Foreword and Acknowledgments viii

I. Not-Working on Yourself

1. 24-Hour Lucid Dreaming. 3
   Dreaming, Mysticism, and Physics

2. Lucidity and Dreamwork 17
   Dissociation, Pristine Consciousness,
   and Lucidity Training

3. Enlightenment, East and West 30
   Multicultural Understanding of Enlightenment

4. Deep Purple Buddhism. 45
   The Teaching of the Abhidhamma
   and the Common Cold

5. Not-Working on Yourself. 65
   Different Realities, Examples of Sentient Healing

6. Reflection, Flirting, and Beeping 79
   Beeping Diagrams, Psychology and Physics

7. Theory and Practice of Divination. 98
   Psychology, Advanced Physics, and Divination

II. Lucid Healing

8. Time Travel 113
   Reincarnation and Stepping Out of Time

9. Lucid Healing, Preventive Medicine. 128
   The Nonlocal Origin of Body Symptoms

10. Touch and Entanglement 143
    Nonlocality between the "Healer" and the "Problem"

11. Addictions and Relationships. 162
    Changing the Atmosphere That Creates Addictions

12. Unbroken Wholeness in Relationships 173
    We Are Very, Very Different and Also the Same

13. Dreaming As World Work 185
    Lucidity and Consciousness in Large Groups

III. Lucid Living

14. Love Story, the Double 199
    The Big You, the Double, and the Little You

15. Panacea for the Tragedy of Being a Person. . . 210
    The Meaning and Timing of Consciousness

16. Diamond Center of the Mandala 223
    *The Ancient Spiritual Practice of
    Becoming a Diamond*

17. Reality as a Magic Symbol 232
    The Political Incorrectness of Dreaming

Bibliography. 239

Index 246

Foreword and Acknowledgments

This book appears in its present form because of my friends. I am indebted to Uncle Lewis (Lewis Obrien) for awakening me to the concept of the Dreaming.

Dear reader, please note, my use of the term "Dreaming" is based on my own work as a therapist and is not meant to explain or pretend to understand the deep and mysterious meaning of "Dreaming" as it is used in the various Australian Aboriginal traditions. My references to "Dreaming" in connection with those traditions are intended to honor and give credit to the significance of those who know and once knew Dreaming as the basis of life. (A percentage of the royalties from this book are donated directly to Australian Aboriginal sources.)

I am grateful to the Process Work Centers of Portland, Oregon; Zurich, Switzerland; London, England; Tokyo, Japan; and Brisbane, Australia for supporting the research and educational procedures found in this book.

I am thankful to Lily Vassiliou of Athens for transcribing the original lectures from which this manuscript has arisen. Leslie Heizer gave wonderful structural advice and was kind enough to help clean up the final copy. Julie Diamond, Jan

Dworkin, Sara Halprin, Lee Jones, Herb Long, Dawn Menken, Max Schupbach and Jytte Vickelsoe were very helpful with the first drafts. Thanks to Nova Development Corporation for permission to use their clipart images.

Jim Chamberlin and Pearl and Carl Mindell awakened me to the connections between this book and the foundations of Eastern and Buddhist thinking, but they are not responsible for my misunderstandings of that ancient subject. What a surprise it was for me to discover that my explorations of physics and psychology had expanded some of the ancient Buddhist themes! I am also indebted to John and Gladys Johnson, who pointed me in the direction Mbiti's African concepts of time, supporting my interpretation of time in physics and experiments in stepping out of time.

Amy Mindell, my friend and partner in all matters, debated, clarified, and co-taught every idea of this book with me. This could easily be called her book as well.

I. Not-Working on Yourself

24-Hour Lucid Dreaming

It was a hot, dry morning in Adelaide, Australia, as Amy and I walked quickly along the river near the university to a conflict resolution meeting we were about to facilitate. We were nervous about that meeting, hoping the Aboriginal people would successfully regain the rights to their land, which had been taken from them by the government.

Uncle Lewis Obrien, an Aboriginal elder with whom we were walking, gently put his hand on my shoulder and quietly said, "Arny, look over there, in the direction of the center of the city. What do you see?" I told him that I saw Victoria Square, the noisy bustling business center of the city. Hundreds of people were shopping; cars honked and buses moved slowly through the traffic. "Looks like a busy city," I said.

Uncle Lewis suggested that I take another look. When I looked again, all I saw was the same noisy city. "Well, your sight is good, but you don't see the Dreaming. White fellas don't see the Dreaming. But they sense it anyhow. White fellas built the center of the city there. We Aboriginal people used to camp where the center is now; that's where the Dreaming is strongest. Victoria Square is a wonderful place;

that's why the modern business center works so well over there."[1]

My environmental consciousness was shocked and enlightened. I realized how my view of the city was filtered through the lens of my U.S. background and education. Until meeting this elder, given the choice, I tended to avoid cities, preferring the countryside. Uncle Lewis made me realize that the miracle of nature I was looking for in the country-side was right in front of me, in the midst of the bustling city. The Dreaming is always present, like an aura shimmering around the objects and events you call everyday life.

Some Aboriginal peoples describe the Dreaming in terms of the dark side of the moon. When the moon is not quite full, you see its bright, illuminated side. You might call it a half moon. But if you look closely on a clear evening, you can see the dark side, silently shimmering next to the more apparent bright side. Like me, most people focus only the bright side and miss the moon's dark face, that is, the Dreaming reality.

The bright side is only that portion of the whole moon that is illuminated. Focusing only on the bright side of the moon and ignoring the dark side might easily make you think that the dark side does not exist, while in fact we need the dark side to represent the whole moon.

Light and Dark Sides of the Moon as Metaphors for Reality and Dreaming

---

[1] In a recent letter, Uncle Lewis explained that Adelaide is built right on the site of the Red Kangaroo Dreaming (Tarnda Munaintya) and that the outline of the outer city streets portrays the outline of that mythic being.

The same is true for everything you see. If you only focus on everyday reality, you neglect the Dreaming. According to Aboriginal thinking, the Dreaming is the basic substance of the material world. The Dreaming gives objects the energy that attracts and repels your attention. If you neglect the Dreaming, you devalue the material environment because you ignore its basis and thus miss half of life.

The power of the Dreaming is right here, behind the everyday world, as part of every object, the part you sometimes forget to notice. From the Aboriginal perspective, everyday reality is the bright side of the moon pointing to the power of Dreaming, the moon's dark side.

In spite of my interest and long background in therapy, dreams, and shamanism, I had unconsciously assumed that the busy city and tall buildings killed the Dreaming. That is probably why, whenever possible, I escaped to the country-side in search of Nature's pristine powers.

Uncle Lewis showed me that the city's reality exists because of the Dreaming. Without it, nothing would be. Dreaming is the energy behind everything; it is the life force of all living beings, the power of trees and plants, and the power of motors, business, and financial centers.

An artist senses the Dreaming in the canvas, paper, and stone and knows that everyday reality is not only concrete. Leonardo da Vinci wrote that artists should look into peeling plaster walls until they can see images emerging from the shapes of the plaster. Similarly, Michelangelo called sculpting a process of bringing out the form that already exists inside the stone. Artists and aboriginal peoples have developed the ability to see the Dreaming, that is, the power behind the figures you see in your nighttime dreams and everyday reality.

ABOUT THIS BOOK

Just as it is my hope that the ruling governments will be more generous in giving Aboriginal people back their land rights, my goal is to make the Dreaming roots of reality so accessible, so visceral, that your conscious mind will give you back your right to dream.

This book is devoted to perceiving, living, and orienting you to the power of Dreaming. We will be taking a journey together, exploring the territory where shamanism crosses the boundaries of physics, where dreams become body experiences, and where everyday life merges with immortality. We will deepen the exploration begun by Freud and Jung into the subconscious or unconscious, which Buddhists refer to as the *Dhammas* and the practitioners of Tantra call the *Void*.

My goal is not to notice the Dreaming only occasionally, but to develop a constant awareness of dreaming. With the new method I call 24-Hour Lucid Dreaming, we will learn to move through and behind the world of everyday life, exploring the world of healing, divination, and immortality.

In the first part of this book, I explore Aboriginal Dreaming and its connections with quantum physics, psychology, and Buddhism. In part two, we will discover the implications of these connections and experiment with new methods of lucid dream and body work, chronic symptom work, relationship and group work.

Part three investigates the implications of the practice of 24-Hour Lucid Dreaming. We will explore how noticing and becoming lucid about the Dreaming connects us to perennial philosophies and to a new self-image. At crucial places along the way, you will be invited to train your awareness in Dreaming. Perhaps you will even consider a whole lifestyle change based on noticing and living the Dreaming, twenty-four hours a day.

THE ONE AND ONLY PROBLEM

It is always foolish to oversimplify complex problems. Nevertheless, from the viewpoint of the Dreaming, regardless of the complexity of your life, you can have only one problem—ignoring the Dreaming background to reality. Ignoring the Dreaming means marginalizing the deepest unformulated experiences that create your actions in everyday life. Every time you ignore *sentient*, that is, generally unrecognized dreamlike perceptions, something inside of you goes into a mild form of shock because you have overlooked the spirit of life, your greatest potential power.

After many years working as a therapist with people from all over the world, it seems to me that ignoring the Dreaming is an undiagnosed global epidemic. People everywhere suffer from a chronic form of mild depression because they are taught to focus on everyday reality and forget about the Dreaming background.

This depression is not the kind that makes you feel miserable. It is subtler than that. This depression is the sense that something in your life is missing even when outer things are going well. Most likely, no matter where in the world you live, many of the people around you feel that something is missing in life, even while they assume that life inherently lacks that special something. As soon as we have a day off, we feel the most common form of this subtle depression; we feel that life is not special but must simply be lived to completion.

While most people hope to do something meaningful, we do not really expect to be totally inspired and awestruck about life on a day-to-day basis. We do not realize that we are out of touch with the core energy of life, with the Dreaming.

Regardless of what our problems appear to be, ignoring the Dreaming reality is the origin of most depression and low spirits. Without Dreaming, you are living only half your life and seeing only half the world.

The simple solution to this global epidemic involves gaining access to Dreaming, in learning to sense the Dreaming in your body's motions and in the signals you send and receive in relationship with the human and natural worlds.

Perhaps you are already trying to solve your mild chronic sense of depression by noticing your dreams, doing meditation, or following a spiritual tradition. These methods are important because they help you find meaning in life. But Dreaming is beyond even meaning; Dreaming is the origin of all your experiences, including your sense of meaning and your deepest beliefs.

DREAMTIME AND PHYSICS

According to Aboriginal Dreamtime traditions, all objects, people, and events are echoes of primal creative forces. Native people everywhere have respected and adored the Earth because they sensed that mysterious Dreaming forces created it. According to one Aboriginal elder, "The flint lives inside this stone like a dream inside your mind. Its essence has been prepared inside the stone since dreamtime."[2]

Present-day physicists think differently. According to what they have been taught, physicists believe that a person observed the stone and consciously decided to create a flint out of it. In contrast to this belief, the Aboriginal elder says that the stone has the Dreaming within itself. Therefore, the stone "interacts" with or "dreams" the hands of the "observer" to bring out the flint-like essence that was already present within the stone. In other words, you do not observe and do things; you are attracted to things and their Dreaming power orients your behavior.

While modern physics and Aboriginal science differ, they also share certain ideas. Indigenous people speak about Dreamtime as the root and essential power from which everything else comes; quantum physicists speak of an invisible mathematical entity called the *quantum potential* from which reality arises.

As you may know, the quantum world cannot be seen or measured directly. As Werner Heisenberg once said, the quantum potential is a sort of "tendency for things to happen." In

---

[2] Robert Lawlor, *Voices of the First Day: Awakening in the Aboriginal Dreamtime* (Rochester, Vt.: Inner Traditions International, 1991), 35.

my recent book, *Quantum Mind: The Edge between Physics and Psychology*, I show how the forces of Dreaming appear in terms of the quantum wave potential in physics.[3]

Let us explore the meaning of tendencies, or quantum wave potentials, by looking at a psychological analogy. Right now, as you sit or lie reading this book, ask yourself what tendencies your body has to move in one direction or another. Do not move yet; just take a moment to feel those tendencies. Now, experiment with letting your body move in the direction of those tendencies. As you move according to your innermost tendencies, notice the movements your body is making. Do they have any significance for you?

The point is that your tendency to move in one direction or another precedes the actual movement. You cannot measure your tendencies, even though you can feel them. Your tendency to move, which precedes your actual movement, is like the quantum wave potential, which is a tendency for things to happen before they occur and can be measured.

For most physicists today, the quantum world is essentially a mathematical dimension whose essence cannot be measured in terms of everyday reality. According to this theory, everyday reality comes from the mathematical dimensions of the quantum world, just as the real world does not exist in Aboriginal culture without tendencies, that is, without the Dreaming.

Most physicists do not let themselves make definitive statements about the quantum world because it cannot be directly measured. Yet some, like physicist Fred Alan Wolf, refer to the tendencies of the quantum potential in connection with the Aboriginal concept of Dreamtime.[4]

---

[3] See the bibliography for the details on this and other books mentioned in the footnotes.

[4] See Fred Alan Wolf's easily read and well-documented *The Dreaming Universe: A Mind-Expanding Journey into the Realm Where Psyche and Physics Meet* (New York: Touchstone, 1995).

Other physicists also speak of a Dreamtime world from which the real world emerges. I discuss elsewhere how astrophysicist Stephen Hawking's new theory of "imaginary time" is a version of Dreamtime.[5] Hawking's imaginary time cannot be measured, yet it is needed to explain what happened at the moment the real universe began.

Other physicists, such as David Bohm, did not speak of a universe that began with imaginary time, but believed instead that the quantum potential is connected to the state of *unbroken wholeness* from which the everyday world arises or *unfolds*. This unbroken wholeness is yet another form of the Dreaming.

In many ways, the Dreaming is to the Aboriginal view of reality as the quantum potential, with its tendencies, imaginary times, and unbroken wholeness, is to the modern physicist's view of reality.

Aboriginal thinking is ahead of physics in that indigenous people insisted that to feel well and enjoy your life, you must perceive and live in the Dreaming. Like many spiritual traditions and individual mystics, Aboriginal spirituality aims at direct access to life in the Dreaming, life in what the native Americans call the Great Spirit.

THE MANY NAMES FOR THE DREAMING

The forces of the Dreaming hidden in matter are the potential, future forms of all things. In this last century, Jung and Freud would have spoken of the Dreaming in terms of the subconscious or unconscious mind. Psychology has become so popular that millions of people today refer to their unconscious as the subliminal origin of their behavior.

In the years since Freud developed his concept of the drives and Jung postulated archetypes within the unconscious, since Erickson introduced his "unconscious"

---

[5] You will find more on imaginary time in my *Quantum Mind*, chapter 36, "The Self-Reflecting Universe."

mind, psychology has reached an impasse in finding out more about the unconscious. Studying Aboriginal Dreaming (as well as Buddhist ideas of perception, which we will look at later) will teach us more about the unconscious. The more we know about this realm, the more we will be able to understand parapsychology, psychosomatic medicine, synchronicity, and perhaps even life itself.

Native Americans, Aboriginal Australians, Taoists, Zen Buddhists, Tantric meditators, and mystics everywhere do not think of the Dreaming world as an "un"-conscious. For these peoples, the sentient Dreaming world is the basic reality. Though marginalized and invisible to mainstream cultures today, Dreamtime has been the essential reality for peoples from the beginning of history.

The energetic tendencies that dream everyday life into existence have gone by many names. Taoists call them "the Tao that cannot be spoken." Chuang Tsu, the ancient Chinese sage, referred to Dreaming as the "Primal Force." Native Americans speak of Dreaming in terms of the power of the "Great Spirit." Tantric meditators speak of the mysterious "Void," and physicists speak of quantum wave functions.

So many spiritual traditions and perennial beliefs support the concept of Dreamtime that you might ask why most of us forget the Dreaming and hang on to everyday reality as if it were the only reality. What hinders us from exploring Dreamtime, our natural inheritance?

I have several answers for why we marginalize the Dreaming and ignore our sentient tendencies, the shimmering sense of the dark side of the moon. First, few people focus on subtle tendencies; there is little community support for doing so. Then, these tendencies are subtle, and their meaning is not immediately apparent. Most people do not think about quick sensations they do not immediately understand. Finally, to catch actions and thoughts as they are arising from the background of subtle tendencies, you must have developed your mindfulness and concentration, which I call lucidity.

An Aboriginal Australian answered the question about why we ignore the Dreaming more simply; he says that mainstream people have simply left Dreaming behind.[6] This man is not only speaking about colonization, that miserable repressive chapter of history in which European civilization dominated and injured Aboriginal Australia. He is also speaking about the internalized racism, the devaluation of Dreaming characteristic of most people in mainstream cultures. He is speaking about how non-Aboriginal peoples everywhere marginalize their own Dreaming. Most of us living in mainstream cultures have learned to turn against and ignore our own Dreaming souls.

Mainstream educational systems repress not only the Dreaming, but the Aboriginal way of life as well. Most school systems reprimand children for being dreamy. As a child, you are in danger of being publicly humiliated if you are meditative or regularly enjoy fantasy.

Everyone, not just Aboriginal peoples, suffers from the decimation of Aboriginal cultures. Today, even though some mainstream people in democratic cultures are awakening to racism, very few notice internalized oppression of Dreaming or its depressing effect on everyone's aboriginal nature. You may be ignoring the Dreaming because of external and internal racism.

The Aboriginal cultures that supported Dreaming have been so hurt by racism that they are just about overwhelmed by Western attachment to "everyday reality." Racism suppresses aboriginal people, their cultures, and everyone's inner tendencies toward Dreaming.

The Nez Perce, a Native American group from Eastern Oregon that became famous because of their heroic and peaceful Chief Joseph, warned that the European work ethic kills Dreaming. "My young men shall never work. Men

---

[6] "White man got no Dreaming, him go 'nother way. White man, him go different." This Aboriginal Australian's words are quoted in David Coxhead and Susan Hiller's *Dreams, Visions of the Night* (London: Thames and Hudson, 1975), 5.

who work cannot dream, and wisdom comes in dreams."[7] For the Nez Perce and other Native American peoples, such as the Maricopa of Colorado and the Iroquois of New York, Dreaming was the expression of the highest divinity.[8] The racism and colonization of Aboriginal and emerging world cultures is the same internalized repression of our own Dreaming souls that happens daily.

At first inspection, native traditions appear to have been decimated. Yet some Aboriginal peoples will tell you that the concept of Dreamtime is undefeatable. Australian Aboriginal elders say that you can kill the kangaroo, but not kangaroo Dreaming. While many of us struggle to protect the land rights of native peoples, Dreaming has its own self-protection. It cannot be destroyed, but is inherent in the land and in everyone's deepest experiences. It is the basic energy of the universe. You can kill people and destroy objects, but the Dreaming, which creates them, is still there. Supporting native peoples and rediscovering access to Dreaming go hand in hand.[9]

24-HOUR LUCID DREAMING

Today, most non-Aboriginal people associate Dreaming with experiences that occur during sleep at night. This understanding of Dreaming was expanded on by the concept of "lucid dreaming," which was introduced in the United States in the 1970s primarily through the work of Stanford University researcher Stephen La Berge, who wrote *Lucid Dreaming: The Power of Being Awake and Aware in Your Dreams*. La Berge defined lucid dreaming as awakening in nighttime dreams and moving about in them while asleep.

---

[7] Ibid., 12.

[8] Ibid., 13.

[9] Readers who are mainly interested in developing conflict resolution techniques may refer to my *Sitting in the Fire: Large Group Transformation through Diversity and Conflict* (Portland, Oreg.: Lao Tse Press, 1995). The present book stresses the inner work needed to do such group work and the lucid living style that can result.

However, according to the Australian Aboriginal peoples as well as to mystics, Dreaming happens all day long in our subtle experiences, which are almost too quick to catch, are irrational and dreamlike, and are difficult to formulate. Dreaming happens all the time, just *before* new thoughts and actions arise.

My first book, *Dreambody: The Body's Role in Revealing the Self*, written in the early 1980s, showed how subtle body experiences and body symptoms are reflected in our nighttime dreams. This reflection shows how dreaming is happening all day long. If you track your experiences closely, you notice the Dreaming showing itself during the day. Every time you feel a bit sleepy, have what you might call an intuition or sudden fantasy, sense a slight moodiness, or feel strange sensations in your body, you are Dreaming in the daytime.

Because you are Dreaming all day long, I wish to expand the idea of lucid dreaming to mean *being awake during Dreaming not only at night but also during the day*. To live and follow the spirit of Dreaming, you need what I call 24-Hour Lucid Dreaming. The Dreaming is a tendency; it is our basic perception that precedes all thoughts and sensations that can be formulated. The Dreaming even precedes the dreams you have at night!

The illustration below shows where lucid Dreaming fits into the spectrum of our waking and sleeping consciousness. You will see the relationship between your different states of awareness, between the deepest unconsciousness to action in everyday reality. At the bottom is the root, the tendencies called Aboriginal Australian Dreaming.

In the center of the picture, arising from the Dreaming, is Dreamland, the events and figures of nighttime dreams. I call this area at the center Dreamland to differentiate it from the Dreaming at the base. In other words, the Dreaming is the power that creates the figures of dreams, and the Dreaming unfolds into Dreamland.

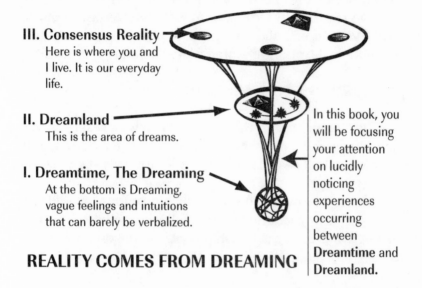

III. Consensus Reality
Here is where you and
I live. It is our everyday
life.

II. Dreamland
This is the area of dreams.

I. Dreamtime, The Dreaming
At the bottom is Dreaming,
vague feelings and intuitions
that can barely be verbalized.

In this book, you
will be focusing
your attention
on lucidly
noticing
experiences
occurring
between
Dreamtime and
Dreamland.

REALITY COMES FROM DREAMING

Finally, at the top of the cone, you see everyday reality, or rather, "consensus" reality with its objects and parts. You can see in this picture how both Dreamland and consensus reality grow out of the Dreaming.

Do not worry about grasping all the details of this diagram, since we will discuss it again later. The point of the diagram is to show the primal action of the Dreaming and to prepare you for training your attention and becoming lucid.

As you grow in lucidity, you notice that everything that catches your attention, *everything*, including sudden flashes, symptoms, relationship issues, and world events, is preceded by tendencies, by the Dreaming. We will discover together how living in the Dreaming means living in a nondualistic world with fewer tensions and less anxiety than you may ever have known.

I have learned this from physics and from Aboriginal wisdom. You can learn it from Buddhism, from this book, and from yourself, tracking your own experiences and living a lucid life. No special abilities are needed. Anyone can relearn how to live in the Dreaming world. The power to gain access to Dreamtime is everyone's natural inheritance.

You must only retrain your attention to perceive tendencies that you can barely formulate in everyday terms. Training your attention will allow you to live in that incredible and awesome reality, the Dreaming power behind everyday life.

 ## THINGS TO REMEMBER

The Dreaming is to the Aboriginal view of reality as the quantum potential, with its tendencies, imaginary times, and unbroken wholeness, is to the modern physicist's view of reality.

When you are lucid, you will notice that everything which catches your attention, *everything*, including sudden flashes, symptoms, relationship issues, and world events, is preceded by tendencies, by the Dreaming.

Lucidity and Dreamwork

The Tao that can be expressed is not the eternal Tao.
The name that can be named is not the eternal name.
"Non-existence" I call the beginning of Heaven and Earth.
Existence I call the mother of individual beings.
Therefore does the direction towards nonexistence lead
to the sight of the miraculous essence.[10]

In the last chapter, I mentioned that 24-Hour Lucid Dreaming is the ability to continuously notice the tendencies that precede events, to be aware of the Dreaming background that gives rise to everyday reality. I will use *Dreaming*, with an uppercase "D," to mean using our sentient abilities to recognize the arising of experience before it has even been able to formulate itself. In contrast, *dreaming*, with a lowercase "d," refers to fantasies or dreams you have at night.

For example, let us say that you are a bit paranoid, that you dream and fantasize that people do not like you. These

---

[10] From Lao Tzu's, *Tao Te Ching: The Book of Meaning and Life*, trans. Richard Wilhelm (New York: Arkana-Penguin, 1986), 27.

dreams and fantasies are dreaming. If you were more lucid, however, and able to do 24-Hour Lucid Dreaming, you would notice how incredibly sensitive, in fact even exquisitely sensitive, you are to certain feelings, as if you were a flower noticing the slightest variations in the wind. This sensitivity is a tendency that precedes your suspicions that others do not like you. The more lucid you are, the more sensitive you become, and thus the less involved you get in the more dualistic experiences of "me" and "them." There is just awareness of sensitivity.

Achieving the depth of experiences characteristic of 24-Hour Lucid Dreaming has been a spiritual goal of many peoples for thousands of years. The Taoists referred to dreams, fantasies, and everyday reality as the *Tao that can be expressed* and warned that it *is not the eternal Tao*. For at least three thousand years, Taoists have spoken of sages who knew the *Tao that cannot be spoken*. We might say that they were speaking about 24-Hour Lucid Dreaming, and about the Dreaming to which Aboriginal Australians have referred.

The ancient Chinese sage Chuang Tsu called the Tao the "primal force." In his words, "there must be some primal force, but we cannot discover any proof. I believe it acts, but I cannot see it. I can feel it, but it has no form."[11]

Patanjali, the legendary yoga master of fourth century India, recommended "witnessing the process of dreaming or dreamless sleep."[12] We might say that he recommended becoming lucid about the sentient experience that precedes ordinary dreams. Shortly thereafter, Tibetan Buddhists devised a method they called "Dream Yoga," which had the goal of being lucid both day and night. In *Sleeping*,

---

[11] *Chuang Tsu*, trans. Gia-Fue Feng and Jane English (New York: Vintage Books, 1974), 24.

[12] See A. Shearer's excellent translation of the original work *Effortless Being: The Yoga Sutras of Patanjali* (London: Unwin, 1989), 64.

Dreaming, and Dying, the Dalai Lama defines dream yoga in Tibetan Traditions as "a practice similar to what is called in the West lucid dreaming."[13]

In Western tradition, lucid dreaming refers to awakening within dreams that are happening while we sleep. In contrast, Dream Yoga has a larger goal that includes 24-Hour Lucid Dreaming, that is, being aware of the sentient states that precede all kinds of thinking and perceiving. Tibetan Buddhist monks refer to this larger goal as "the Great Awakening."

As we saw in the last chapter, present-day and ancient indigenous traditions see the everyday world as a kind of flower rising from the dreaming Earth. Historically, a person did not need a special calling to notice that reality arises from the dreaming Earth; this practice belonged to everyone's development and belief system.

For example, according to the Nai-mus-ena people in South America, ordinary reality began as a dreamlike fragment of the their great deity.[14] Likewise, early Indian philosophers thought the world came from the Dreaming power of the great god Brahma.[15]

The Native American Hopi called their creator, "'A'NE HIMU," a "Powerful Something" who created all manifestations. Note that this powerful "something" has no direct verbal counterpart in everyday life. It is a power of the universe that creates the entire real world.

You may recall the picture at the end of chapter 1, which shows how consensus reality grew out of dreamland and Dreaming. It appears again below.

---

[13] See the Dalai Lama's wonderful mixture of scientific and spiritual thinking in *Sleeping, Dreaming and Dying* (Boston: Wisdom Publications, 1997).

[14] Coxhead and Hiller, *Dreams*, 4.

[15] Ibid, 7.

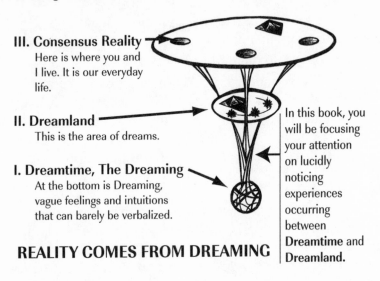

III. Consensus Reality
Here is where you and
I live. It is our everyday
life.

II. Dreamland
This is the area of dreams.

I. Dreamtime, The Dreaming
At the bottom is Dreaming,
vague feelings and intuitions
that can barely be verbalized.

In this book, you
will be focusing
your attention
on lucidly
noticing
experiences
occurring
between
Dreamtime and
Dreamland.

REALITY COMES FROM DREAMING

Level III consensus reality, or "CR," is at the top.
Dreamland consists of nighttime dreams and fantasies you
might suddenly have during the day. Dreaming is the root of
all things. It is Chuang Tsu's "primal force" or the "Tao that
cannot be said," the Australian Dreaming, the Brahma, the
"Powerful Something," and the Native Americans deities
that personify the Dreaming.

In the Hopi world, everyday reality is already manifest;
thus real objects are part of the past. In other words, the
Hopi concept of past is the present for everyone else
because, according to Hopi thinking, the present everyday
reality is the result of experience that has already unfolded!
The Hopi do not refer to past, present or future, but instead
speak about the present and past in terms of "that which is
manifest." The future is "that which is beginning to manifest." The future is a Dreaming that has not yet unfolded.

Sentient, nonconsensual experience is a tendency that
has not yet manifested in terms of everyday conceptions.
With 24-Hour Lucid Dreaming, you notice the Dreaming,
notice flickering signals such as sudden feelings you cannot
explain. This experience is further from everyday awareness,
and for most of us living in mainstream cultures, requires
retraining awareness to be able to perceive these signals.

As we know from the last chapter, according to the Australian Aboriginal people, nothing can exist in everyday reality that does not exist in the Dreaming first. Aboriginal cultures encouraged tribespeople to notice the Dreaming in the present, because being in touch with the Dreaming assured a safe future.

Music is very close to the Dreaming.

In some tribes, the first thing a person does upon waking is to wander alone into the bush or along the seashore and create a song based on the dreams of the previous night. They believe the animals and birds hear the dream being sung and recognize that the singer is in touch with the inner world, and therefore they assist him or her in daily hunting and gathering.[16]

Modern spiritual teachers from India, such as Sri Ramana Maharshi (1873-1950), stressed the importance of living close to the Dreaming, to the state he called the "natural life," the oneness that precedes duality. The Indian parallel to 24-Hour Lucid Dreaming is the *sahaja samadhi* of Hinduism. The *Encyclopedia of Eastern Philosophy and Religion* defines the Sanskrit term, *samadhi* as "a state of consciousness beyond waking, dreaming, and deep sleep," and *sahaja* as "the natural state."

Another Indian spiritual teacher whose teachings involved Dreaming was Sri Aurobindo (1872-1950), the Indian nationalist and mystic philosopher who underwent a spiritual transformation while imprisoned for suspected terrorist acts in 1908. He emerged as a great teacher by suggesting various methods for becoming lucid in the divine natural state that gives rise to life.

LUCID DREAMING

Until now, Western approaches to lucid dreaming have focused on becoming lucid in dreams that occur during the

---

[16] Lawlor, *Voices of the First Day; Awakening in the Aboriginal Dreamtime*, 38.

night rather than on the Dreaming itself. To this end, modern spiritual teachers such as Rudolf Steiner have studied various aspects of lucid dreaming. In the 1970s, Alan Worsley in Britain and Stephen La Berge in California both learned to dream lucidly (at night) and created scientific breakthroughs in the study of dreams. They discovered how rapid eye movements, or REMs, indicated that dreaming was occurring.

Rapid eye movements mirror the motions of the dreamer's eyes. If you look up in a dream, the eyebrows on your face move upward while you slumber. REMs can be traced on EEGs, or electroencephalograms. With training, for the first time in the history of science, people could report from the world of dreams (through their REMs) while still dreaming! Thus, the Western concept of lucid dreaming became associated with awakening in a dream.[17]

24-HOUR LUCID DREAMING

In recent times, the Dalai Lama pointed out that Tibetan yogis develop lucidity first in meditation, then in their dreams, and finally in deep, meditative states during everyday reality. The Dalai Lama called attaining such lucidity "the Great Realization."

---

[17] Recent research from dream psychologist Jayne Gackenback extends La Berge's concept of lucid dreaming. In her conversations with the Dalai Lama in his *Sleeping, Dreaming and Dying* (pages 101 and following), Gackenback defines new aspects of awareness in addition to lucid nighttime dreaming. She speaks of "witnessing dreaming," as a peaceful inner awareness or wakefulness completely separate from the dream. "In witnessing dreaming, it's said that the person can manipulate the dream, but simply has no wish to do so. . . . Finally, I want to introduce a third state called witnessing deep sleep. This is described as dreamless sleep, very like a non-REM condition, in which you experience a quiet, peaceful inner state of awareness or wakefulness—a feeling of infinite expansion and bliss and nothing else." Gackenback goes on to say that lucid dreams can emerge out of any dream, and that "emergence is self-reflection."

According to the Dalai Lama, the Great Realization is a "pristine consciousness," which can manifest in waking consciousness without the practitioner being actually absorbed in meditation. It is sometimes said to occur "between thoughts; it is . . . the basic, primordial nature of consciousness itself. . . . As such, it is the basis for all mental content."[18] This is yet another perennial description of what I am calling 24-hour Lucid Dreaming.

YOUR EXPERIENCE OF DREAMING

Thus far, I have been referring to various teachings about 24-Hour Lucid Dreaming to illustrate the universality of interest in Dreaming and its basic connection to spiritual traditions.

Soon, in order to understand 24-Hour Lucid Dreaming, you will have a chance to explore your own experience of Dreaming. But first, let me say a bit more about how Dreaming appears. Dreaming expresses itself in your awareness, in everything you notice. It expresses itself in your everyday experiences and in terms of your dreams, fantasies, and sentient, not-yet-verbalized experiences.

When these Dreaming experiences begin to manifest themselves, they appear as subtle or flickering nonverbal sensations, moods, and hunches, which cannot be easily translated into words, and which you rarely understand with your everyday mind.

Next, Dreaming appears in your awareness as signals, ideas, and perceptions that persist and no longer flicker. You probably label these "signals, ideas, and perceptions" as

---

[18] The Dalai Lama goes on to say, "In Tibetan dream yoga practice, one method used is to instruct the sleeping person softly, 'You are now dreaming'" (p. 103 of his text, *Sleeping, Dreaming and Dying*). In the glossary of that book (p. 231), he defines the dreambody and dream yoga. "Dreambody. The apparent physical form one has in the dream state. In the yogic practice of the stage of completion within the Highest Yoga Tantra, the dream body is cultivated as a simulacrum of the illusory body."

aches, pains, dreams, and thoughts. The main difference between these experiences and the earlier subtler, flickering sensations is that these persisting perceptions can be formulated in terms of everyday language.

Thus, Dreaming shows up in at least two ways:

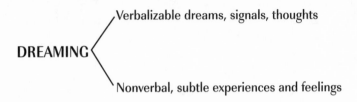

If you are like most people, you probably focus most of your attention on your verbalizable experiences such as observations, ideas, and dreams. To perceive more subtle nonverbalizable experiences and feelings, you may need retraining, or re-minding. "Re-minding" means reflecting on the mind you already have!

In spite of Dreaming's universal significance as the basis of consciousness, you probably skip it because the cognitive part of your mind cannot immediately grasp its significance. The Tao that cannot be spoken is indeed just that—nonverbal. You cannot know ahead of time exactly what the vague experiences of the Dreaming mean. Therefore, in the following experiment, you should ask your cognitive mind to be patient and relax so that your attention can have experiences before they can be comprehended.

Feel free to explore, to do research, and to pay close attention to your experiences. I would like to suggest that you read and answer the following questions, sentence by sentence, exploring your inner experience for the next few minutes. Having a pencil and piece paper at hand is useful. I hope you enjoy this self-exploration.

RESEARCH INNERWORK

Beginning with where you are now sitting or lying, scan your body and your feelings; gently question yourself about your experience. What sensations are you feeling right now? Can you put them into words? This requires your ordinary conscious awareness.

Now ask your cognitive mind to relax for a minute. Relax and take a breath. When you are ready, search your experience and check on other feelings you may have, feelings that have not yet been formulated. It might help you to be unknowing, clouded, and open. Sensing subtle feelings develops your "pristine consciousness," that is, your lucidity.

Be patient with your awareness of this unformulated region of your experience. Give yourself time to explore. Being as lucid as possible, notice nonverbal experiences. Imagine you are a researcher exploring an unknown region of life. Perhaps you notice relaxation, or jittery feelings, or excitement.

Now go further, notice and follow these subtle sensations as they change, unfold, or turn into images or other feelings. To do this, just focus patiently, gently, and exactly on those subtle experiences. Hold them and quietly notice how they evolve. Give them time; they will reflect on themselves, emerge, and explain themselves in terms of pictures, sounds, movement, stories, songs, and so forth. Make a note about the events that you are noticing. Now that these events are unfolded in terms of images or ideas, do you have a hunch about their possible meaning?

Next, ask yourself about recent dreams. Do you recall a recent dream? If not, consider the last dream you can remember, even if it was years ago. Who was in it? What were you doing in that dream? Do you remember what the atmosphere felt like in that dream?

Now, let us do a new kind of dreamwork. Recall the results of Dreaming, that is, of lucidly exploring your subtle experiences. Are the experiences that came from your subtle sensations somehow formulated in your dreams? Guess where the subtle sensations might fit into your dream. Are they in the background of the dream, or do they appear directly in the dream as one of its figures or events? In what way do your subtle sensations explain your dream?

Being lucid about your dreamlike tendencies and sensations may give you a hint about your life right now, about who you are and how to orient your everyday life to your dreaming. Try to sense these hints about who you are and your direction in life. What do you need to do to live closer to those sensations?

In this short exercise, you explored those tendencies that Lao Tzu called "the Tao that has not been spoken." You may have noticed how your deepest, almost unformulatable experiences and tendencies give rise to understanding the images in your dreams.

The point is that Dreaming is the root of reality. Being lucid helps you understand dreams and may even be helpful with comprehending some of your body sensations. In other words, by becoming lucid about the Dreaming in the form of feelings and body sensations, you get a new view on dreams, and perhaps on some of the mysterious experiences you have been having in everyday life. Take a moment and think about your everyday life. Think about what it means to be lucid about the Dreaming, about subtle tendencies and how these might reorient you.

As you go further in this work, you will notice how increased lucidity enriches your sense of everyday life. As you learn to move backward and forward from the Dreaming to reality, you will be able to sense how everyday life arises from Dreaming and how Dreaming is a magical symbol for a mystical reality.

DISSOCIATION FROM DREAMING

Lucidity teaches you that the origin of your thoughts, observations, and dreams is happening right now, in the background of everyday consensus reality. As you become more lucid during the day, you can predict what you are going to think, dream, and do before you go to sleep at night.

Perhaps the only reason nighttime dreams sometimes seem so difficult to understand is that you usually do not pay attention to tendencies, vague sensations, hunches, feelings, aches, and pains. You notice the Dreaming only when it gets to the point of unfolding, only when a body sensation already hurts. You probably pay attention to your ideas only when they are almost formulated. The more lucid you become, the more you will note your experiences *before* they reach the level where they can be clearly felt, thought about, and remembered.

The psychological reason for ignoring the Dreaming is that you learned to separate yourself from these elementary tendencies, sensations, preverbal feelings, and thoughts. Thus today you tend to neglect and dissociate from whatever you cannot comprehend with your ordinary mind.

In other words, dreams are difficult to understand not because they are naturally mysterious, but because you have dissociated yourself from their source. From our developing perspective of lucidity, dreams are the products of Dreaming, just as a tree is the result of a seed in the ground.

After discovering that lucidity explains dreams, some people may wonder if nighttime dreams stop as you become more lucid during the day. Not at all. Your dreams will not stop. Rather they seem to become clearer. In other words, dreams do not disappear as you become lucid; they become more comprehensible.

A PERSONAL EXAMPLE

One night while I was beginning this book, I dreamed I was traveling to a town called Livingstone. When I awoke next morning, I made an association to that place. To the name "Livingstone," I associated a stone, a living stone, the stone of the alchemists. The stone was the goal of the essence of their work, the *Opus Magnus*, or Great Work. Its purpose was to gain immortality or become stonelike, that is, unchanging and free of time.

As soon as I recalled these associations to the word Livingstone, I thought, Ah ha! That's it! Livingstone is a part of me, the immortal part; it is a place I am traveling to. Now I understood my mysterious dream. It is about the path I am on, about this book. My dream is about immortality, the part of us that is free from time and social pressures.

Associating to dreams is one of the most powerful and popular methods we have for understanding dreams. About a hundred years ago, Freud and Jung showed us how to associate to dream images, and this powerful method may go back even further in time.

The question we might ask at this point is this: why do we need to associate to a dream to know what it means? Another way of asking this question is: how did you get separated from your dreams in the first place? Why did I need to associate to Livingstone to understand the dream?

The answer to this question comes from experience; you dissociate yourself from Dreaming by marginalizing tendencies because they are too vague, too incomprehensible for your ordinary mind. If we did not dissociate ourselves from Dreaming, we would not have to associate to our dreams to discover their meaning. This leads us to another question: in my dream of Livingstone, what exactly did I dissociate myself from? What was the Dreaming behind my dream of Livingstone? What was the seed of that dream?

The evening before the dream I was feeling very relaxed, very "stoned," a sensation that lingered into the next day. The vague sensation behind the dream is a feeling of timelessness and detachment. I ignored that feeling and thus the dream reminded me of it, and of the Dreaming experience behind the dream image called "Livingstone."

Until now, much psychotherapy and dreamwork has been about the process of reassociating yourself to feelings and actions that became split off from your everyday mind. Our new concept of 24-Hour Lucid Dreaming moves the concept of therapy closer to spiritual practice. Instead of associating to dreams, we can learn how to contact Dreaming before it gets dissociated, thus learning to understand dreams even before they occur.

24-Hour Lucid Dreaming means becoming aware of every moment, noticing subtle feelings, the seeds of reality, *before* they unfold and become differentiated into the parts that appear in dreams and symptoms.

THINGS TO REMEMBER

According to the ancient Chinese sage, Chuang Tsu, the Tao was "the primal force." He said, "There must be some primal force, but we cannot discover any proof. I believe it acts, but I cannot see it. I can feel it, but it has no form."[19]

Dreaming first appears in everyday life as flickering nonverbal sensations, moods, and hunches. Later it appears as persisting signals, ideas, and perceptions, as verbalizable dreams and visions that can be expressed in terms of everyday language.

If you dissociate from the Dreaming, you need to associate to dreams.

---

[19] *Chuang Tsu*, 24.

THREE

Enlightenment, East and West

In Buddhism, "Enlightenment" means "a final blessed state marked by the absence of desire or suffering." [20]

In chapter 2, we saw that Stephen La Berge's work on lucid dreaming gave rise to the Western concept of lucidity. For La Berge, lucid dreaming meant becoming aware of yourself while dreaming at night, noticing you are dreaming while in a dream. He pointed out that you could use lucid dreaming to interact with figures, avoid nightmares, and solve problems.

24-Hour Lucid Dreaming expands the concept of lucidity by encouraging you to become aware of the entire pre-dream state—the vague field of experiences that occur *before* you even have a dream. I propose a new meaning for lucidity: awareness of the source of dreams, awareness of the Tao that cannot be spoken.

---

[20] From *Merriam-Webster's Collegiate Dictionary*, electronic edition, 1.5, 1994-96.

Until now, lucidity meant sensing in a dream that you are one of a group of figures, events, and objects. From now on, I would like lucidity to include knowing you are dreaming in nighttime dreams and also sensing that you are dreaming even before dream figures arise in the night.

The following two diagrams portray these two different meanings. On the left, the entire circle, with all the figures, is meant to represent your nighttime dream. On the right, you see your dream again, but this time the entire circle area is shaded. The shaded area represents the subtle sensations and feelings in back of the dream, the sentient experiences that give rise to the dream. Your ordinary, everyday self is represented in both pictures by the figure in the inner circle.

Your self

Lucidity's Original and New Meaning

On the left, you are lucid about being in a dream.
On the right, you are lucid about the Dreaming, the sentient (shaded) area which gives rise to the dream.

In the original meaning of lucid dreaming, the first picture on the left, you are a figure running around, aware of yourself and of other figures in a dream.

In the picture on the right, in the new meaning of Lucid Dreaming, you no longer identify with only yourself, but rather with all the Dreaming that gives rise to the figures in the dream. One of these dream figures is the everyday you. Your new identity, however, is with the sentient experience behind the dream, which cannot be quite formulated in words. Thus you identify with the sentient, subliminal feeling (the entire shaded area) that gives rise to the dream and all of its parts, including, of course, your little self.

In the new meaning of Lucid Dreaming, you sense the vague sensations of the Dreaming and identify with these sensations. If you think of these sensations as a kind of soup, your new identity is the fluid part of the soup as well as all the figures, including the little you.

AN EXAMPLE

Let us take an example to help understand the new meaning of 24-Hour Lucid Dreaming. One night, a client of mine who had been feeling quite well suddenly became frustrated when his computer software no longer worked properly. As soon as his computer began making trouble, he felt himself becoming tense. He soon got so angry that he felt like throwing out his computer. He had a choice of either ignoring or noticing this frustration, even though it lasted only for a short period of time.

Because we had been working together on lucidity, he caught himself choosing to separate himself from his frustration. That choice did not make him feel better; it merely marginalized his discomfort, and he felt worse.

To make the story short, after cursing his fate for a moment, he realized that to solve the computer problem, he needed to be patient with his sense of frustration, not put it aside or marginalize it. He said, "I decided to stop skipping over everything. I tried to feel that frustration and experience its unformulatable roots. This had the paradoxical effect of relaxing me so that I could actually fix the problem. As it was already late in the evening, I went to bed."

That night he dreamed of a hyperactive child who had become furious because she had somehow broken her bicycle. He calmed the child and fixed her bicycle. When he awoke in the morning, he instantly understood his dream because he had been lucid about the sentient experience of his frustration the night before. The child and her bike were symbols of his own frustration at having to learn to use his computer. He was aware of the Dreaming before having a dream.

In the diagram to the right on the page 31, the figure is aware of the Dreaming field, the frustration and calming, as well as the interactions between the other dream figures and himself. As you become lucid about your sentient, almost nonverbalizable experiences, you begin to see through the eyes of what we might call the dreammaker, your sentient experiences. From this viewpoint and experience, you have a sense of something awesome moving you and you see the various figures that unfold from that sense. Lucidity gives you insight into life, the insight of the power of Dreaming.

I love dreams and have fun exploring and investigating them. Here in this book, our goal will not be to interpret dreams, not to become lucid in dreams, but to know their significance before they occur.[21] Our goal will be 24-hour Lucid Dreaming. When you are lucid, you notice your normal little self, and also a bigger self, a Big You, the entire field and feeling around you.

The only reason you do not see and live through the insightful mind of your bigger self all the time is that your little self feels sentient experiences are unnecessary, incorrect, or incomprehensible. If you are interested in developing increased lucidity, I suggest that you focus on your feelings of being well or unwell, exhausted or anxious, depressed or angry. Rather than taking substances or drugs to reduce these feelings, focus on your awareness. Do not support the food or drug industry that helps you marginalize Dreaming and the Big You.

Marginalizing means that something that was in the center of your awareness—like frustration or tiredness—is placed in the "margins" of your focus where you can barely see it. See the diagram below.

---

[21] For methods of dream interpretation, see my forthcoming book, *The Thoughts of God and the Meaning of Dreams* (to be published).

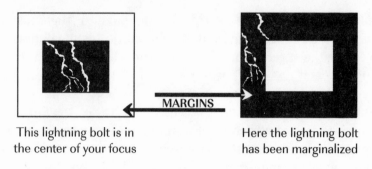

This lightning bolt is in   Here the lightning bolt
the center of your focus   has been marginalized

Marginalization is a deep process, which usually occurs without you even noticing that you have done it. Of course, you can suppress experiences, but to do that, you need to know they exist. Marginalization is subtler; you need mindfulness, concentration, and training to notice how Dreaming gets put into the margins of awareness.

Buddhism has long suggested developing "bare attention," which means becoming aware of *everything* you experience, including the arising of your experiences. As psychology expands, it too will learn to become lucid, which reverses marginalization. Through opening up to everything that you experience, you get to know your total Self. Knowing what you experience, the pond, and all the fish in it, you detach from only being one of the little fish and begin to identify with all the other fish as well as with the process of change itself.

DIFFERENT LEVELS OF REALITY

As we saw in chapter 1, your experiences can be understood in terms of three different realms, which are not firm and fixed with clear boundaries, but which flow into one another. Realm I is the Dreaming world. Realm II is dreamland, which includes the dreams you recall from the night. Realm III is consensus reality, the everyday world.

Dreamtime or Sentient Reality

Here you notice deep experiences, normally disregarded feelings and sensations that have not yet expressed themselves in terms of meaningful images, sounds, and sensations. These disregarded or marginalized feelings are sentient, that is, preverbal, feelings and sensations.

Dreamland

In dreamland you notice dreams, fantasies, figures, and objects while awake or asleep. You can formulate these experiences more readily in words, in contrast to the experiences of Dreaming, which can barely be grasped in everyday terms.

Everyday Reality

In everyday reality you may use your ordinary attention to notice and share your observations of yourself and others, objects, and ideas. Everyday reality can be described in terms of time and space in contrast to Dreaming and dreamland, whose times and spaces are vastly different from those of everyday reality.

While most dreamwork strives to understand the content of dreams from Realm II and relate them to everyday reality, or Realm III, 24-Hour Lucid Dreaming focuses mainly on the sentient Realm I, the root of reality.

NOTES ABOUT NEW TERMS

You may have noticed that I am using certain words in a special way. Perhaps you do not normally use terms such as "sentient" or "lucidity" or "Dreaming," or perhaps you use them to mean something different than their meaning here. I apologize for using old terms in a new way, since it may be complicated to learn new terms or use old ones in a slightly new manner.

I have tried to retain older terms as much as possible but have had to develop new meanings for older terms because the older words frequently marginalize the Dreaming and sentient background to reality. I hope you can share my experience of words; they are important only insofar as they point back to experiences that can barely be formulated.

For example, I redefine the term "consciousness." According to *Webster's* dictionary, consciousness is a state of being aware of something within oneself or of something external. It means "mind" or the "upper level of mental life of which the person is aware in contrast to unconsciousness."

I would like consciousness to mean something more specific, namely the ability to observe parts of consensus reality and parts of dreams and to understand these parts as aspects of your self. In this new definition, consciousness deals with parts and with their connection to one another.

"Sentient" is another important word. It refers to the continuous and automatic awareness of subtle, normally marginalized experiences and sensations. Everyone is sentient. According to some Buddhists (such as Thich Naht Hahn) and most Aboriginal people, everything, including stones and trees, is sentient.

If you become aware of your sentient experience instead of marginalizing it, you are lucid. Lucidity means awareness of sentient experience, which precedes everything you think, see, hear, and do. Lucidity leads to a new viewpoint about life, to the wisdom or insight of Dreaming. When you are lucid, you sense tendencies as well as actualities.

Later in this book I will show that the difference between lucidity (of sentient experiences) and consciousness (of parts) is a cornerstone of a new psychology that connects spiritual, meditative, and Aboriginal traditions with socially oriented, parts-oriented thinking. Lucidity deals with sentient experience, while consciousness is connected to everything that unfolds from sentient experience.

Lucidity and consciousness are different levels of awareness. Most of us are either lucid and live in the sentient world or conscious and focus on everyday events and social issues. I use the term "enlightenment" to mean simultaneous lucidity and consciousness, that is, having a sense of the origin of all things and simultaneously living with full awareness of the amazing diversity of this world.

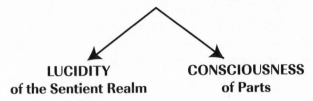

ENLIGHTENMENT=Awareness of Awareness

LUCIDITY
of the Sentient Realm

CONSCIOUSNESS
of Parts

Though individual teachers vary, Eastern meditative rituals often stress lucidity. Western psychology refers to sentient experiences as the "unconscious" and focuses instead on "consciousness" as I am defining it here.

In contrast to my use of the term enlightenment, most students of Buddhism and other religions of Indian origin refer to enlightenment as a state of mind in which you have gone beyond desire and suffering to attain bliss. The greatest teachers do not support just leaving the world, but support living in the here and now as well.

For example, Sri Ramana Maharshi speaks of a kind of relaxation that comes from living close to the dreaming. He says, "the *samadhi* I speak to you about is different. It is *sahaja samadhi*. You realize that you are moved by the deeper Real Self within and are unaffected by what you do or say or think. You have no worries, anxieties, or cares, for you realize that there is nothing that belongs to you as ego and that everything is being done by something with which you are in conscious union."[22] Maharshi goes on to say that this *samadhi* is not a withdrawal from the world but a full life within it.

Samadhi is a kind of enlightenment similar to my present definition. Becoming lucid of the sentient level of experience opens up the possibility of existence outside the everyday reality of conflicts and polarization while simultaneously

---

[22] These words come from *The Teachings of Ramana Maharshi*, edited by Arthur Osborne. (Samuel Weiser, New York.) Thanks to Jim Chamberlin for awakening me to Maharshi's work.

being aware of the problems and polarization, diversity, and tension of the everyday world.

"East" and "West" have long been used by the West to refer to Asia on the one hand and the United States and Europe on the other. These terms are no longer valid in psychology, because each of us has both "Eastern" and "Western" (as well as Northern and Southern) aspects, regardless of where we live.

Still using the old East-West axis, let me say that the Western thinking is mainly cognitive; it trains us to think in terms of parts and supports "individuality." In contrast, so-called Eastern orientations usually view developing your sense of individuality within a group as a sign of unconsciousness. If I stand out or speak up as an individual in Eastern traditions, others might consider me in need of learning more about feeling the group atmosphere.

There is no firm Western and Eastern psychology; both are points on a wide spectrum of human experience. What I am calling sentient awareness is closely linked to traditional Eastern, African, South American, and Aboriginal attitudes toward awareness. This awareness is interested in oneness, in the subtle experience and interconnectedness of all things, in the similarity between things, and in feeling related to all things.

In contrast, Western traditions often focus on strengthening the little you, or the "ego." The focus is on valuing your identity and difference or relationship to others. When you are in a Western mode of awareness, you tend to marginalize sentient experience, and when you are in an Eastern mode, you tend to marginalize the sense of being an individual in the midst of a field. As a result, you might marginalize yourself and others who are not the leaders. See the diagram below.

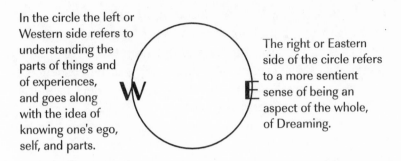

In the circle the left or Western side refers to understanding the parts of things and of experiences, and goes along with the idea of knowing one's ego, self, and parts.

The right or Eastern side of the circle refers to a more sentient sense of being an aspect of the whole, of Dreaming.

Both forms of awareness are important. Combinations of them create the beauty and diversity of cultures in our world. How each of us defines and feels about reality determines who we are and where we wish to live. Without an overview of the diversity of awareness, people in an Eastern or Western mode of experiencing life may have a difficult time understanding one another. The Western orientation inside of you thinks the Eastern side cannot be clear and definitive, while the Eastern or Southern mode finds the Western mode destructive to the feeling of interconnection.

The Japanese Buddhist Rinzai Zen sect of Japan has a sentient view of reality, summed up by the expression "Every day is a fine day."[23] For the typical Western mind, this sounds very mysterious. In the present terms, since everyday reality manifests sentient experience, every day is a chance for lucidity, for sensing the whole as it unfolds. Thus "every day is a fine day" refers to a lucid world of experience that lies beyond the duality of good and bad, right and wrong.

From a strictly Western mode of experiencing things, every day is definitely *not* a fine day. In a Western sense, some days are lousy because you are one part of the field and another part of the same field might be troubling you.

Both viewpoints are important because, if you go back to your sentient experience, what seems "bad" or "wrong" to

---

[23] I am indebted to the Zen Master and lead Roshi of the Rinzai sect in Japan, Keido Fukushima Roshi, for this information.

your "little self" is, from the larger viewpoint, just the field, your Bigger Self making you aware of its various forms. From this viewpoint, life itself is unfolding in its incredibly diverse way. The essence of events, their sentient essence, is neither good nor bad, but rather awesome, deep; it is prior to the concepts of good and bad.

From the "Big You" viewpoint, Zen is correct. "Every day is a fine day." At the same time, if you are not in contact with that sentient aspect of reality, for the little you, some days can be just terrible!

When you are in an "enlightened" mood, regardless of what tradition or country you come from, you can say, "this day is fine," and mean that it is both fine and at the same time just terrible. For example, say some illness threatens you with the end of life. The little you feels this situation is terrible. Yet, if you go deep inside, if you find the sentient experience in the background, if you are lucid, some amazing experience or story will emerge.

Consider the story of someone who broke her foot. How can breaking that foot be "a fine day?" When I asked the woman who broke her foot to go into the essence of the feelings of her broken foot, she became lucid. She said the field around her foot wanted stillness, no movement, no walking. By meditating on the broken foot and the "seed" or essence that had unfolded into that broken foot, she discovered that she could not walk, but also that she did not want to walk! In contrast to her normal everyday attitude, she now discovered that she disliked going out of her house. She loved the quiet that had been trying to reach her awareness earlier but that she had marginalized.

Thus every day is a fine day; the broken foot is a fine foot! And, at the very same time, the day she broke that foot was horrible. The way you view life is a matter of awareness and viewpoint. From the viewpoint of the little you, life is good or bad. From the viewpoint of the Big You, the sentient you, every day is perfect.

ZEN TIGER

One night, when Amy and I were talking about enlightenment, I created an extension of a classical Zen story. It made me laugh, and I hope it will make you laugh too. Here is the story, with my additions.

A Zen student goes to her Zen class and asks the teacher in front of all the students, "Would you explain the meaning of life?" The Zen teacher says, "Yes, when there aren't so many people around."

The next day the student comes again after all the other people in the room have left and says, "Now that everybody has gone, would you explain to me the meaning the life?" And the teacher says, "Too many people present!"

From the sentient viewpoint, there are too many people around, that is, too many parts focusing on consciousness. When the student went back to her teacher a second time, even though there were no people around in consensual reality, there was still too much everyday consciousness.

The point is that too much of the ordinary person is still there. Too much of the consensus reality person is looking for parts and answers. The person asking about the meaning of life is too focused on ordinary life. In this sense, there are too many people around.

After thinking about this story for a few minutes, a new possibility emerged in my mind. I imagined that the Zen student underwent a spontaneous enlightenment; she became lucid and conscious. Suddenly, she understood her teacher. Furthermore, she became aware of the marvelous diversity of parts in her field, the student and the teacher and the "too many people."

She not only valued the Big Self but the small self as well and said, "Thank you dear teacher, but neither of us should suppress consensus reality. Our little selves are the ones who long for the necessary teaching. Furthermore, since you and I are part of the sentient essence of all things, perhaps you and I are both students and teachers as well as the 'many people'!" Hearing this, the open-minded teacher's eyes opened wide as he bowed before her.

After I told this story to a friend, he offered another story in return. His version of a different Zen story goes like this:

A man was having a bad day. While he was walking along the road, a tiger appeared out of nowhere and chased him to the edge of a cliff. He jumped but caught a little vine as he was falling. Looking down he saw a bottomless abyss below him. Looking up he saw the drooling tiger waiting over his head! Our poor man looked in front of him and saw a mouse chewing away at the root of the vine he was holding! Right next to that vine, he also saw a wonderful strawberry and said, "Oh, how beautiful!"

I love this story too. The man in the story is very detached from the "parts" view of reality, and from the disaster threatening his little self. Even though death threatens his little self from above, below, even though there is nothing to hold onto, he notices the strawberry in front of him. Instead of marginalizing that little strawberry, he sentiently experiences it and goes into a state of bliss, despite the fact that his consensus reality situation appeared bleak. He detaches from everyday reality, from the outcome or future of the little self, by focusing instead on the unfolding of moment, the Dreaming of that strawberry![24]

From a consensus reality viewpoint, you might think he was crazy. But for the man hanging onto the vine that is being chewed away, the fate of his little self is not important. His security lies in Dreaming, the unfolding of what catches his attention. Enlightenment is his awareness of the dreaming strawberry as well as the tiger above him and death below. But from the consensus viewpoint, this story is not a sign of enlightenment but of utter madness!

In any case, if our man was sentient to begin with, he might have sensed the tiger coming at him before it got there. In that case, he would have noticed some weird

---

[24] The strawberry is a symbol of immortality in Native American traditions.

indescribable feeling, become lucid about his own tendency to roar and be angry, and realized his own powerful nature. He would have unfolded that sentient roar and embraced the entire field, including his little self, his fear of death, the angry tiger and the strawberry of immortality.

Therefore, even before the tiger started to chase him, before the tiger had a chance to move, the man would have growled like a tiger. In this case, both he and the real tiger might have seen each other but would not have been interested in looking at each other again. In any case, the man in the original story chased by a tiger tried to follow his sentient experience, and he did so once at the cliff edge even though you and I might have hoped he would have done so earlier.

Lucidity is probably what the ancient Chinese sage Chuang Tsu meant when he said in the fourth century B.C., "If one is true to one's self and follows its teaching, who need be without a teacher?"[25]

Chuang Tsu's viewpoint is that everyone has a true teacher, the sentient field, the Tao that cannot be verbalized. In fact, if you think about it, you and I have the same amazing teacher as everyone else. In a way, there is one guru, the primal, sentient force of Dreaming, which has a thousand faces. We are all students of the same teacher, and in a way, are different faces of the same student.

Chuang Tsu teaches that following one's true Self is the greatest teacher. It is best to know this teacher. What else could help if a tiger is about to chase you?

 ## THINGS TO REMEMBER

24-Hour Lucid Dreaming means identifying with the sentient essence that precedes dreams and real events.

Marginalization means that something takes what was in the center of your awareness, such as frustration or

---

[25] *Chuang Tsu*, 26.

tiredness, and places it in the "margins" of your focus, thereby ignoring it.

The term sentient refers to the automatic awareness of subtle, normally marginalized experiences and sensations. Everyone is sentient, and according to some Buddhists and most Aboriginal people, everything, including stones and trees, is sentient as well.

From the "Big You" viewpoint, Zen is correct. "Every day is a fine day." At the same time, if you are not in contact with that sentient aspect of reality, for the little you, some days can be hell!

It is best to follow your true teacher, your own true Self. Who else could help if a tiger is about to chase you?

FOUR

Deep Purple Buddhism

Vast indeed is the ultimate Tao,
Spontaneously itself apparently without acting,
End of all ages and beginning of all ages.
Existing before Earth and existing before Heaven . . .
In the East it taught Father Confucius,
In the West it converted the "Golden man"
(the Buddha).
Taken as pattern by a hundred kings,
Transmitted by generations of sages,
It is the ancestor of all doctrines,
The mystery beyond all mysteries.[26]

This ancient quote suggests that the Tao, the Dreaming, precedes everything and is the parent of all spiritual teachings. The Tao, as the ancestor of all doctrines, created the Buddha's teachings about the deep, sentient experiences of meditation, and all other religions and traditions, including Western science.

---

[26] From *The Tao* by Philip Rawson and Laslo Legaza (London: Thames and Hudson, 1979), 8, originally on the Ming rock (1556).

In comparison to ancient Aboriginal science and to Taoism, which emerged three thousand years ago, Western psychology is a mere one-hundred-year-old baby. Freud wrote his first papers on the interpretation of dreams around 1900. Only in the last thirty years have the structural components of perception been understood in terms of channels and signals in psychotherapy.[27] Knowledge about the manifestation of sentient experience in terms of parts and processes is just beginning, and there is much research to be done within the Western way of understanding behavior in terms of parts and specific processes. It too must be unfolding from the Dreaming.

In contrast to modern science, knowledge of sentient aspects of awareness has been available for several thousand years in Asia. The application of such knowledge in therapy is just beginning. The long history behind Hinduism and Buddhism has much to offer modern psychotherapy, and the wisdom of these traditions has not yet been fully tapped within contemporary psychology.

STAGES OF PERCEPTION IN BUDDHISM

Thus far we have seen different stages of perception, including Dreaming, dreamland, and everyday consensus reality. To notice dreaming experiences you need to be lucid. Then you can track them as they unfold into dreamland and into everyday consensus reality, or CR.[28]

Everyday reality in the West and in most big cities of the world suppresses Dreaming whose timing is not linear.

---

[27] The development of Western psychotherapy is strongly linked with modern science. For example, signal and channel concepts arose in part through the study of information processing in electrical engineering.

[28] Recall that the concept of "reality" is a cultural concept, not an absolute truth. I have been using the term CR to refer to the implicit, consensus reality of a given group. In the present book, written with a multicultural population in mind, CR means cosmopolitan reality. This CR marginalizes sentient experience.

Altered states of consciousness and foggy dreamlike states belong to nonconsensus reality, or NCR. While the altered states of NCR are also real, there is no consensus on the reality of dreamlike experience, which is considered subjective or internal. Nonconsensus reality includes dreamland, which has parts and images, and also the sentient realm, which is nonverbal experience. CR is the world of experimental physics, where you can measure signals and make observations. From the cosmopolitan view, consensus reality seems more objective, NCR more subjective.

I. Dreamtime 〕 NCR, Nonconsensus Reality
II. Dreams 〕
III. Everyday Reality 〕 CR, Consensus Reality

To understand how our nonverbal, sentient experiences unfold into dreams and everyday reality, we need to differentiate the above scheme of perception. One such differentiation can be found in the ancient Buddhist text called the *Abhidhamma* or "higher teaching." Written in the third century B.C., the *Abhidhamma* contains philosophical, psychological, and doctrinal discussions and classifications.[29]

If you are unfamiliar with Buddhism, you are surely going to ask why I would relate the teachings of this ancient text to your own dreamwork, to your everyday reality. Why study something so apparently foreign to what you know? The answer is that the *Abhidhamma* can teach you more about your ability to perceive Dreaming in terms of sentient

---

[29] "Buddhism," *Microsoft Encarta 97 Encyclopedia*. Microsoft Corporation, Seattle, (1996). All rights reserved. The *Abhidhamma Pitaka* consists of seven separate works. They include detailed classifications of psychological phenomena, metaphysical analysis, and a thesaurus of technical vocabulary. Although technically authoritative, the texts in this collection have little influence on the lay Buddhist. The complete canon, much expanded, also exists in Tibetan and Chinese versions.

experiences. We will discover in the following chapters that lucidity will enable you to solve personal, physical, emotional, and even political problems you thought were hopeless.

Buddhism's *Abhidhamma* can be most helpful in solving these problems because it adapts easily to changing conditions and to a variety of cultures. Furthermore, although Buddhism is philosophically opposed to materialism, it welcomes modern science. In fact, it holds that the Buddha applied the experimental approach to questions of ultimate truth.[30]

The *Abhidhamma* analyzes hidden details of the process of perception, explaining that a trained meditator can track between seventeen and forty-five specific steps, or "moments," during the process of observation. These steps precede your hearing or seeing anything.

According to this ancient text, a complete perceptual process such as hearing the sound of an object, knowing what it is, or seeing and recognizing it, occurs in steps. British psychologist Brian Lancaster refers to Buddhist scholars who illustrate perception in terms of the experiences of a sleeping man.[31]

My rendition of this example goes as follows. Imagine a person sleeping under a fruit tree and slowly awakening. The wind rustles the branches above him, causing a piece of fruit to fall and graze the man's ear. He is aroused from sleep, senses the fruit, and eventually eats it.

The *Abhidhamma* breaks this process of noticing and eating the fruit into seventeen steps. The first eight stages of perception happen while the man is sleeping. During sleep he notices the wind rustling in the branches and the fruit falling to the ground nearby.

By the time he has reached the stage in perception in which he is aroused from sleep, he has already passed through

---

[30] Ibid.

[31] See Brian Lancaster's excellent *Towards a Synthesis of Cognitive Science and Buddhist Abhidhamma Tradition*, 124-28.

the first eight stages of perception. In the next nine steps, he recognizes and eats the fruit. These nine final steps include picking up the fruit, "receiving" it, "examining" it by squeezing and smelling, and recognizing what it is. He "establishes" it as fruit and finally "registers" it.

This example is analogous to what happens each time we notice anything. In its earliest stages, observation consists in being awakened to the existence of an object that you will eventually observe. Later on in the process of observation, you begin to notice the object, decide what it is and whether you will look at it, and finally, observe it.

The diagram on page 50 provides an adapted summary of the Buddhist stages of perception. The seventeen different stages of perception fit into the broad categories of Dreaming, dreamland, and consensus reality.

DREAMING OR SENTIENT PERCEPTION

I call the first eight stages *sentient perception*, because they occur without the presence of your ordinary conscious mind. Your body notices and responds to outer events without any conscious participation from your mind.

The first "moments" of perception consist of a disturbance to your unconscious mind; in fact, the first step is called "disturbing the unconscious mind." Then there is a sense that something occurs called "turning toward the sense door." In other words, after your unconscious mind is disturbed, your senses begin to function. Next comes a sensation of awakening to something, but with no recognition of the object at this stage. This stage is "characterized by a sense of contact between the sense organ and the sense object. One sees an object but does not yet know anything about it."[32]

According to the *Abhidhamma*, the earliest stages of perception are characterized by being awakened and determining whether something is agreeable or disagreeable

---

[32] Ibid, 126.

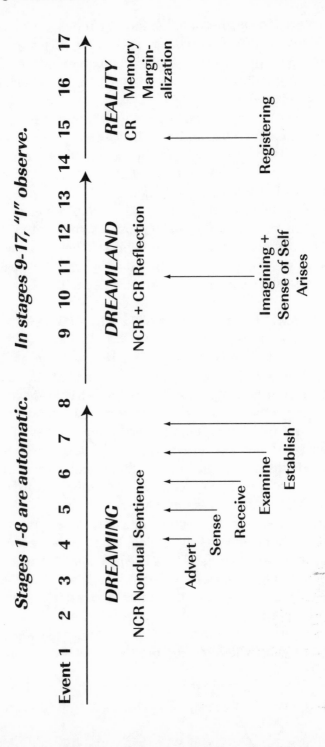

STEPWISE EVOLUTION OF PERCEPTION IN THE *ABHIDHAMMA*

Stages 1-8 are automatic.

In stages 9-17, "I" observe.

Event 1 2 3 4 5 6 7 8   9 10 11 12 13 14 15 16 17

DREAMING   *DREAMLAND*   *REALITY*

NCR Nondual Sentience   NCR + CR Reflection   CR Memory
                                                Margin-
                                                alization

Advert
Sense
Receive
Examine
Establish

Imagining +
Sense of Self
Arises

Registering

to your unconscious mind. This is then followed by what the *Abhidhamma* calls "examining," that is, labeling things. At this point, the nature of the object is assessed. It is present, but there is no everyday reaction yet. Associations to the sense object are examined here. Then comes "establishing," which determines a response to the object, although you are still not intelligently aware of the object. All these perceptual processes have been more or less automatic.

DREAMLAND

In the next nine stages, consciousness arises. In the first six of these nine stages, there is a vague sense of "I." This is the moment when you yourself are awakening and your everyday self is becoming vaguely aware that the object you will look at exists.

Next comes a perceptual stage the *Abhidhamma* calls "running." Here you discover and evaluate whether the object to be seen is the same or different than yourself, and you form an aversion or attachment to what you see.

At this point, you appreciate objective significance for the first time. You begin to think about your experience of the object as if it were only outer reality. Habitual ways of seeing things come in and your sense of self as a subject is generated.

CONSENSUS REALITY

Finally, you "register" the fact that you have had a perception. This is translated from Buddhist teaching as "having the same object." In this stage you feel that you can reflect and remember the object. This is the beginning of what we call short term memory.

I have categorized the Buddhist perceptual system into the broader areas of Dreaming, dreamland, and everyday reality below.

You can see in the diagram on page 50 that the first stages, Dreaming, are totally automatic. Your "I" is not present but is "sleeping," or unconscious. That "I"—that is, the little you that you normally identify as the perceiver—does not appear in the Buddhist scheme of perception until after stage eight.

At this point, Dreamland begins and your "I" begins to function. It likes, dislikes, or ignores events. This is the point at which you remember or reject fantasies and dreams. Your "I" is associated with resistance or "edges" to experiences. Events that seem too far away or unimportant are blocked here and do not go on to be "registered" in everyday consciousness.

If you were the person sleeping under the fruit tree, you could say,

1. You are sleeping and your head is covered;
2. and 3. A breeze blows, fruit falls from the tree near your head;
4. You are aroused from sleep by the sound;
5. You remove your head covering and sense;
6. Your hand picks up the mango;
7. Examining happens by squeezing;
8. The fruit is recognized by its smell;
9 through 15. You decide you like the fruit and eat it;
16 and 17. And savor its aftertaste.[33]

Without meditation training, no one notices all of these stages. According to Buddhist scholars, with training, you can become aware of literally billions of such moments that are said to occur with lightning speed.

THE POWER OF OBJECTS AND EVENTS

Why is it that even after extensive training, we never seem to notice certain things? According to the *Abhidhamma*, the things themselves did not have sufficient

---

[33] My itemization more or less follows that of Lancaster, 1997.

power to reach consciousness. In fact, events are categorized in terms of their power. This power determines
whether or not they reach everyday awareness. There are
three power categories: very slight, slight, and great.

In other words, "you" are not totally responsible for
whether or not something reaches your everyday awareness, because the objects or events themselves have power
and contribute to your awareness. This way of thinking is
similar to the Aboriginal idea that all the things of this world
are imbued with the Dreaming that unfolds into everyday
observations.

The point is that you alone do not perceive; all
perception, including intuitions, sudden flickering thoughts
and sensations, "co-arises," or participates in "your"
perceptions.

To make the teachings of Aboriginal science and
Buddhist analysis useful to therapy, I will rename the very
slight, slight and great powers in terms of marginalization
and edges.

Marginalization:

During stages one through eight, *very slight* objects do
not arouse you from your unconsciousness of them, or, you
may experience them sentiently but do not recall them later.
These objects do not have the Dreaming "power" to reach
your dreams or fantasies, yet your body senses them.
Because the sensations are too weak, too foreign to your
mind, or too uncomfortable, they are marginalized. Stages
one through eight of the *Abhidhamma* are moments when
marginalization occurs. Something about you, let us call it
your body, notices an event, disagrees, and has an aversion
to it.

The *Abhidhamma* says simply that the event was very
slight. For example, in your sleep, perhaps your hand
pushed a mosquito away, but you do not remember that
mosquito.

That sentient, marginalized mosquito experience was a
dhamma. According to the Venerable Nyanaponika Thera,

in his *Abhidhamma Studies*, "Unlike the persisting persons and objects of everyday reality, the *dhammas* are evanescent occurrences, momentary mental and physical happenings . . . with the sole exception of the unconditioned element, *Nibbanna*, or liberation."[34]

I call these evanescent occurrences, these momentary mental and physical happenings, "flirts." Events flirt with us in the first stages of awareness, but if we are not attentive to their occurrence, they get marginalized and do not reach our everyday awareness. To notice events, or flirts, in the first eight stages, we need lucidity. In other words, the Dreaming power of a very slight event is a combination of the nature of both the observer and the event itself.

Edges:

Slight objects get to the point of being "established." This means that they reach the stage where the "I" arises and perceives. While slight objects get beyond stage eight, they are too foreign or disagreeable to your identity to be focused on and remembered.

Many of the first symptoms of stress are slight objects. You feel slight discomforts that get past the barrier of marginalization, but they are so uncomfortable or disturbing to who you are that you may choose to ignore them. These flirts just do not seem to fit into your everyday reality, or they seem too insignificant to focus on. They are like dreams you forget. They do not reach everyday awareness because of an "edge" or barrier between who you are and these "not-you" experiences.

Edges make life seem more comfortable. For example, someone bothers you, but you repress it because you think you should not be upset by that person.

---

[34] See his clear and simple exposition, Venerable Nyanaponika Thera, *Abhidhamma Studies, Buddhist Explorations of Consciousness and Time* (Boston: Wisdom Publications, 1998), xvi.

Suppression:

Great objects are events that make it to the surface of your everyday observation, past marginalization and edges. They have the power to "force themselves" on your awareness, even if you were not sentient and even if you have edges against them. Like a symptom that hurts, you are pressed to notice and remember this event but can still decide to *suppress* it.

Let us say, for example, that something hurts, depresses, or upsets you. Even though you try to ignore it, you cannot help knowing about it. It hurts too much. But instead of focusing on it, you go to the movies, eat, or take an aspirin. This is suppression.

You should notice that the *Abhidhamma* does not place responsibility for what is perceived entirely on you, the perceiver, nor on the object or problem arising in your mind. Rather, the object's power, its very slight, slight, or great nature plays a role in determining your ability to observe it.

SELF-CRITICISM AFTER THE HAIRDRESSER

Here is another example of marginalization and edges. When Amy, my partner and wife, was in the mountains a couple of months ago, she felt something bothering her, but did not know what. She marginalized the feeling because it was too subtle to pay attention to.

Her body felt low; she felt unusually tired. For Amy, the sense of "feeling low" at this point was a very slight object in the Buddhist way of thinking. The feeling did not have the power to completely manifest, even in her dreams. If you had asked Amy if anything was bothering her, chances are she would have said that everything was fine. While she somehow sensed that something was bothering her, she could not have said what the problem was.

While hiking one evening, Amy decided to become more lucid. She used her trained attention to overcome marginalization and meditated on herself, focusing on the subtle nonverbal experience of "feeling low."

As she focused on her Dreaming, she recalled what seemed to be a ridiculous memory. She remembered that a thought about her hair had "flirted" with her earlier. She had been to the hairdresser and had a few blonde streaks put into her brown hair. Once she was in the mountains, however, she felt that her blonde streaks make her look "too much like a city woman." After she recalled the thought that had flirted with her earlier, she realized that it was what was depressing her. She decided to accept this very slight event and even go further. She got over any edges she had to thinking about that "damn yellow streak" in her hair and the people in the mountains who might not like it.

Amy pondered this conflict and arrived at a startling insight. She said that the Dreaming behind the "people who lived in the mountains," who might not like her hair, was a native American spirit, a powerful sense about the power of the mountains and the earth. "Ah ha," she said. "Now I remembered another idea that flashed by my attention. When I looked in the mirror earlier that day, that yellow streak in my hair looked a bit Native American! Wow, there was no real conflict. The Dreaming behind the mountain people and the yellow streak in the hair was one and the same, the Native American's powerful way of being."

Amy said she was feeling that power, but had been marginalizing it until then. In other words, the event that made her feel low was the subtle conflict she felt between the native mountain people and her city self. The Dreaming behind those people was the same as the Dreaming behind the blonde streak in her hair: Native American, the sense of the earth's power. She told me that as soon as she realized this she felt a lot better; she remembered her true Self.

The moral of the story is that we forget quick fantasies, such as Amy's fantasy about her hair, because they are very slight, that is, too far away from and too antagonistic to our consciousness. Amy had edges to noticing and remembering what seemed to her a superficial problem.

Often subtle feelings are difficult to work with because of marginalization and edges. Self-criticism or a lack of self-love is not the main problem. From the viewpoint of Dreaming, the basic difficulty is a lack of lucidity.

Training awareness in the sentient realm can, with lucidity, reveal the roots of just about any problem. By focusing on the vagueness of the sentient experience, you become lucid. It is important to remember that behind any apparently outer or superficial difficulty is a powerful Dreaming trying to reveal itself.

The Buddha might say that interrupting what I have been calling marginalization is a prerequisite for arriving at the wisdom state and alleviating pain and suffering. If he were here today he would suggest that you train your "bare attention" to become lucid about sentient experience.[35]

Traditional Western psychology focuses on personal change by developing awareness in dreamland, by removing edges through discussion and dreamwork. Shamanism, bodywork, and Buddhism overcome marginalization with lucidity, or bare attention to the flashes and flirts of sentient experience.

EXAMPLE OF WAKING UP

To understand more about the difference between marginalizing and edges, consider waking up in the morning. Pretend that you have a partner nearby. The alarm clock rings. You sense it, hear it, but you "edge it out." Although you know the alarm is ringing, you feel that you do not have

---

[35] The first chapters of the venerable Nyanaponika Thera's *Abhidhamma Studies*, "For wisdom or insight to arise, the meditator must learn to suspend the normal constructive, synthesizing activity of the mind responsible for weaving the realms of immediate sensory data into coherent narrative patterns revolving around persons, entities, and their attributes. Instead, the meditator must adopt a radically phenomenological stance, attending mindfully to each successive occasion of experience exactly as it presents itself in its sheer immediacy. When this technique of "bare attention" is assiduously applied, the familiar world of everyday perception dissolves into a dynamic stream of impersonal phenomena, flashes of actuality arising and perishing with incredible rapidity."

to obey its command. That alarm clock is not for you. And so, without thinking further, you shut it off. It was a very great object. You could not marginalize it; its ring got over the edge to your ear, but finally, you suppressed it.

Did your partner hear the clock? She tells you later that morning that she did *not* hear it. However, if you set an electrical measuring instrument near her body, you could have seen that her body reacted to the alarm. She had a sentient experience of that clock, but marginalized it.

The *Abhidhamma* would say that for her, the clock was very slight. Her body marginalized it. In other words, the alarm flirted with her, that is, it almost caught her lucid attention. While she may have registered it on a sentient level, as we all register even very slight events, she was not lucid about the clock; it did not reach her lucid awareness.

Does the clock have very slight or very great power?

Now let us imagine another morning with a new set of circumstances. Imagine that this time your partner awakened seconds before the alarm went off and happily got up, turned off the clock, and got you out of bed. According to the *Abhidhamma*, that clock had very great power for her.

In this second scenario, we cannot differentiate your partner's lucidity from the power of the clock. All we can say is that the event had great power. She sentiently experienced that clock even before it rang; her body sensed the alarm "in her Dreaming." The clock went along with her identity as someone who wanted to get herself out of bed;

therefore, she did not "edge out" the clock, but got out of bed. This was an enlightened act on her part. She was mindful, phenomenological, lucid, and finally conscious of the existence of the clock and the need to get up.

The arising of that clock in her conscious mind made it through marginalization and edges, and because of her enlightened attitude, you had to wake up too.

This example shows that the power of an object depends in part on the potential observers. The power of the clock may be very great for one person and very slight for someone else. Furthermore, from the viewpoint of Dreaming, there are no observers to begin with, and thus we can only speak of the power of the overall event flirting with your awareness.

In conclusion then, from the sentient viewpoint, it is "nature," or events themselves, that create marginalization. Whether an event has slight or very great power depends on the combination of the dreamers involved, in our case you, your partner, and the alarm clock. Nothing is independently weak or strong.

With lucidity training, however, you can reverse marginalization. During Dreaming, you sense things but cannot say what they are because perception is clouded and vague. Unless you are lucid, "you" are not perceiving or doing things in this area—they simply happen. The more lucid you become, the more you can function as a participant in Dreaming, together with all other sentient beings.

In Buddhist teachings, it is important to become aware and dissolve attachment (or aversion) to both good and bad stimuli, noticing them and letting them pass on as part of the impermanence of nature. The Buddhist *Abhidhamma* does not wish to annihilate the little self but, as I understand the teaching, to increase the perspective on what the "I" amounts to.[36] The phenomenological teaching of the *Abhidhamma* suggests

---

[36] The total understanding of this "I" from the Western viewpoint is never quite explained. However, the lucid viewpoint gives us insight into this mysterious "I." When you are in a sentient mood, you can experience that the little you or "I" arises from sentient experience as part of the Big You.

that you catch yourself trying to make sense out of things and pay attention instead to that undifferentiated and unified sense of the world from which all things arise.

CONSCIOUSNESS IS REALLY UNCONSCIOUSNESS

Western ideas of consciousness refer mostly to knowing yourself and your parts. However, *from the 24-Hour Lucid Dreaming viewpoint, such consciousness looks like unconsciousness.* Trying to make sense out of perception using only yourself and consensus reality makes you unconscious of the Dreaming, the bigger You, the total field of sentient perceptions.

In other words, the struggle for understanding and consciousness can make you unconscious of sentient experience. Let me explain this in terms of a brief cold I got when I was giving classes on the *Abhidhamma.* My cold began with a very "drippy" experience. Actually, it began in Dreaming as a sentient experience of quietness and inwardness, which I had marginalized some days earlier. By the time my sentient experience of quietness unfolded into having a cold, several days had passed. One night, I was unable to sleep because my dripping nose kept waking me up. Finally, in the midst of the night, I decided to stop marginalizing the disturbing features of my cold and sat up in bed trying to use my "bare attention" and become lucid.

I began to explore my cold with as much sentient awareness as I could muster at that late hour. I felt the sensations in my nose and sinuses. Beneath the sensations of dripping and sneezing, somehow, the sentient essence of that cold reminded me of something like the color purple. Since I was trying to explore the cold sentiently, I did not think, "why purple?" but continued on without trying to make sense of it. Noticing this color, I slipped into a purple domain, a purple world. I was a bit nervous at first; it was foreign to me. But then I decided to follow my awareness as it sentiently "felt" its way around in this purple world.

For some unknown reason, my exploration relieved my sinuses, and they dried out enough to let me go to sleep. I woke up the next morning remembering a dream about a bright purple pharmacy. Parked outside the beautiful purple building was a purple sports car! I immediately understood my dream.

That purple car symbolized the purple experience of my cold. The purple sports car gave me a purple "trip," so to speak. The purple pharmacy in my dream was the purple healing experience. As soon as I woke up in the morning I knew what that dream was about because of my sentient experience the night before.

If I had focused only on the dream and done a more ordinary kind of dream work on that car and pharmacy, I might have asked myself "What do I associate to the pharmacy?" My response might have been "healing," or alternative methods in healing.

To the sports car I might have associated "zooming around." Thinking in terms of associations would lead me to understand my dream as a healing trip. Thinking in terms of associations and interpretations is interesting; it gives meaning to my cold. The dream and associations make sense of my Dreaming.

But such dreamwork thinking has a side effect. *It takes me away from the Dreaming, from sentient experience.* It is very helpful to think in terms of dream parts; in these terms, you can say that the sports car is a symbol of my healing trip and the pharmacy is my body's healing ability. You can say that the dream says, "I'm becoming aware of these parts of myself." That is interesting. It makes me conscious.

But such consciousness *makes me unconscious* of the Dreaming, of the sentient feelings I was having, which are the basis of dreaming. Consciousness would make me marginalize the drippy nose.

If you marginalize sentient experience, *the interpretation of dreams can make you unconscious.* I love interpreting dreams and I do it all the time. Yet I am aware that from another viewpoint, interpretation can make me unconscious of my sentient Self, of the Big Me, that is, the purple world that includes the pharmacy, the sports car, and my dripping purple nose. Being sentient and noticing that deep purple experience made me ecstatic, which is a different-feeling experience than interpreting the dream.

As I write the term, "deep purple," I notice a song begin to arise in my head. What's the name of this song? "Deep Purple." How does it go? Something like, "Deep Purple, over garden walls . . ." That is a very romantic song. The beautiful words and romantic tune of that song bring back my sentient experience. The sensations of the song almost make me lose track of what I am writing just now. Songs describe the indescribable. They bring me back to the "purple" Dreaming, and perhaps only now, with the romantic nature of that song in my heart, do I comprehend my dream. Getting to that sentient, romantic feeling was the point of that cold, and getting to that Dreaming was healing.

You can see from this example that becoming lucid by focusing on sentient experience is very different than focusing on the meaning of the dream. Consciousness of parts can make you unconscious of your sentient experience and discourage you from being lucid.

In contrast to lucidity of not-yet-formulated experience, consciousness—in the way I have defined it—stresses awareness of parts of yourself and your environment in such a way that you can relate to these parts and to others. Consciousness gives you meaning, but focusing only on consciousness of your parts can make you unconscious of Dreaming.

Conversely, being only lucid, as I just was when remembering the song "Deep Purple," can make you unconscious of everyday reality, the world of duality and parts. Lucidity is a trip! You can easily get so attached to it that you begin to lose track of (or look down on) everyday life.

Thus both consciousness and lucidity are important. Lucidity is awareness of the dream's entire premeaning sense, which, when unfolded, leads to the meaning of the parts of the dream. Consciousness values the parts and seeks meaning and interconnection between them, but easily ignores the awesomeness of the Dreaming that is prior to the concept of meaning.

Let me express the momentary effects that consciousness and lucidity have on one another in picture form. Let lucidity be represented by a circle ◯ and consciousness by a square ☐.

Furthermore, let the darkened circles and squares areas refer to focusing mainly on lucidity or consciousness. See the diagrams below. On your left, you can see how lucidity blocks out consciousness. On the right, you can see how consciousness can inhibit lucidity.

**Lucidity Momentarily
Blocking Consciousness**

**Consciousness
Blocking Lucidity**

Enlightenment consists of those moments when you are both lucid and conscious. In the present context, enlightenment means valuing sentient experience and the parts of everyday life, that is, simultaneous lucidity of the sentient realm and consciousness of parts. See the diagram below.

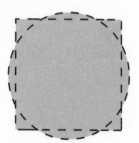

**Simultaneous Lucidity of Sentient Realm and
Consciousness of Parts**

This diagram, consisting of the melding of a square and a circle, represents a combined, multilevel focus consisting of lucidity of the inexpressible feelings and consciousness of the parts and figures that unfold out of these feelings.

 ## THINGS TO REMEMBER

A trained meditator can track "moments" during the process of observation and notice how these events arise and decay.

According to ancient Buddhist teachings, there are seventeen steps, or "moments," preceding your feeling, hearing, or seeing anything.

To make the teachings of Aboriginal science and Buddhist analysis useful to therapy, I speak of the very slight, slight, and great powers of objects in terms of marginalization, edges, and suppression.

Enlightenment means simultaneously valuing lucidity of the sentient realm and consciousness of parts.

FIVE

Not-Working on Yourself

A good cook changes his knife once a year because he cuts, while a mediocre cook has to change his every month because he hacks.[37]

A good cook does not force or work against her food when she is cooking. According to Chinese Taoists, she does "not-doing." Her hands know the Tao of the turkey, where to avoid bones. She is lucid about her sentient knowing of where to make her cut, where and where not to slice the turkey. She follows the path that nature provides.

Cut, Don't Hack This Turkey

---

[37] *Chuang Tsu*, 55.

The cook in an ordinary state of mind hacks, presses, and pushes. She works hard and exerts more energy than the state of mind that does "not-doing." In a Taoist mood, the cook is sentient; the turkey gets cooked as if it were cooking itself.

Becoming lucid of sentient experience while doing things depends in part on the dreaming power of what you are working with, as well as its weight, size, and consistency. In the Buddhist scheme of things we saw in the *Abhidhamma,* all events have power. You will recall from the last chapter that, without training on the part of a person, slight objects do not reach consciousness, while great objects do. Objects have a certain degree of power to interact with you and eventually reach your consciousness. Australian Aboriginal thinking also ascribes power to objects. One man says that we must look at certain trees because their power makes us look at them.[38]

NOT-DOING IN PHYSICS AND PSYCHOLOGY

In principle, according to Aboriginal thinking, anything you can observe has the power of the Dreaming. We saw in chapter 1 that Dreaming is to the everyday reality of an Aboriginal person as the quantum wave potential is to observation in physics. When these wave potentials self-reflect, observations occur.[39]

In other words, if you can perceive something, it has interacted with you in Dreamtime.[40] An object is capable of

---

[38] This man is quoted as calling the power of a tree that catches our attention, "Wayrull" (Salome Schwarz, unpublished dissertation, Union Institute, Cincinnati Ohio, 1996).

[39] I point out in *Quantum Mind* that modern physics agrees with Aboriginal ideas in many various ways.

[40] In my *Quantum Mind,* I point out that the quantum potential is a mathematical formula that reflects upon itself, thereby making observations in consensus reality possible. However, for modern science, whether or not objects are sentient must remain a mathematical hypothesis at this point, because this subtle form of interaction between observer and object cannot be empirically checked.

being seen because it has subtle, generally unrecognized signals producing the sensation of sudden glimpses, flashes, sensations, undefined moods, tendencies, and impulses in you. Although you may think that you are observing and doing things, actually, if you are lucid, you notice that you observe things *in connection with* their observing you.

Anything you observe arises through the sentient participation of everything involved. When you notice this Dreamtime interactional experience, you are lucid; you are doing what the Chinese call "not-doing."

"Not-doing" is a sentient relationship act, an almost magical procedure. Premonitions, moods, and sensations co-arise in connection with everything involved and always precede conscious observation, insight, or everyday events. You may marginalize this co-arising. Perhaps you think that premonitions are projections from the consensus reality (CR) viewpoint. But from the nonconsensus reality (NCR) viewpoint, both you and the events you perceive are part of the Big You.

The meaning of events cannot be known by your everyday mind until they are unfolded into dreamland. From the CR viewpoint, all sentient events are initially meaningless. They get meaning through unfolding into dreamland and consensus reality.

The basic structure of all observations is at first not-doing. You do not do it, you do not observe. It happens! From the consensus reality viewpoint, the sentient basis of observation is called by various names, such as magic, telepathy, or clairvoyance. When you are lucid, you sense the seeds and tendencies of things and divine the future. You sense things moving as if by themselves. From the CR viewpoint, you seem to be involved in "telekinesis"; others may think you move things at a distance. Yet "you" do not do anything. Things just happen!

THE PLUM EXAMPLE

A personal example comes to mind. I recall going for a run with Amy one warm springtime afternoon. As we ran, we shared dreams and spoke about ourselves. At one point, Amy paused to catch her breath as we began running uphill. A flickering impulse suddenly occurred to me, but the impulse was so absurd that I marginalized it. Then, when I caught that marginalization, I decided to let the impulse unfold.

My impulse was a tendency to pull something out of Amy's head! I focused on my impulse, not yet telling her about my tendency to draw something out of her head. I looked at her to see if she was doing something to make me have this impulse, but could find nothing.

I focused on that flash or "flirt," that impulse to pull something out of her head for a moment, and then I shared it. "Amy," I said, "excuse me, but I have a strange impulse to pull a large plum out of your head."

Arny   The Plum   Amy

To Whom Does the Plum Belong?

To my surprise, she laughed so hard she had to stop running. She was happy I had shared my fantasy with her and said that a plum was in one of the forgotten dreams she had the night before. In her forgotten dream, she was playing with a plum. She had forgotten that until I shared my lucid experience.

WHO IS THINKING?

In this example, though I was barely lucid of Dreaming, of the sentient background to events, I was nevertheless able to notice the plum image that I almost marginalized because it was a "very slight" event. But after it flirted with me a couple of times, I caught it. Perhaps it was not so slight after all.

When you are lucid, hidden events rise to the surface. Of course, events are not really hidden; rather they are submerged, embryonic, waiting to be unfolded. It is as if the Big You is reflecting on itself. When "it" reflects, you experience yourself at first being flirted with, and then, as being invited to observe something else. Later on, you think that "you" did the observing, yet the little you is just a witness.

Neither Amy nor I could tell where that plum-flirt came from, whether it belonged to Amy or me. Lucid experience of dreaming occurs before it is broken up into parts, before you know whether it is coming from you or me, or from specific dream images and signals. Lucidity allows you to sense how observations co-arise from everything involved. As lucid experience unfolds, you notice it unfolding and become conscious of figures, motion, parts, and the "other." If you are not careful, you then think you are relating to the other person or to an object. You think you must work consciously on that relationship. That is not a bad idea, but you should also notice that relationships arise, they happen to us. Their basis is not-doing!

To use a musical analogy, consciousness involves writing or knowing the notes of a song, while lucidity is awareness of the feeling background that gave rise to the song.

INNERWORK WITH SONG LINES: THE NOT-DOING OF SONG WRITING

You might enjoy experimenting with the following innerwork exercise that explores not-doing, as well as the difference between lucidity and consciousness in song writing.

Take a moment to ask yourself what you are feeling just now. What words describe your present feelings?

Now, take a moment and ask yourself to feel things that cannot be put into words, or that have not yet been put into words. Focusing on these feelings encourages you to become lucid about sentient, Dreaming experiences you are having just now.

What sound emerges that mirrors your sentient experience? What melody and words would express or almost express your experience? Allow this tune and words to become a song.

Experiment with creating or telling yourself a story in which your song plays a significant role.

That is the not-doing of song writing. You did not quite write that song. It got written, so to speak. You did 24-Hour Lucid Dreaming to become aware of the sentient background in the moment. Then you became conscious of its parts by hearing the tune and finding words. The song is the CR expression of the atmosphere in the Dreamtime background to the present moment in your life. Your song and story have arrived in consciousness. To go further in understanding the meaning of the song, ask yourself about the possible significance of your story.

Some Australian Aboriginal groups speak of "song lines," much as Taoists speak about the "way" or the Tao. Your song line is your present path in life. Give yourself a few minutes to meditate on what it means for you to follow the momentary path symbolized by your story.

THE NOT-DOING OF SWEEPING UP

You can apply not-doing to anything, including cleaning your apartment. Check out how that happens. For example, you may notice your broom "flirting" with you. Then if you become lucid of this sentient experience, you notice the dirt on the floor is flirting with you as well. You, the floor, and the broom are in the midst of a relationship triad. Suddenly, sweeping the floor happens.

Cleaning up becomes a relationship between the broom, the floor and, at the same time, yourself. Your ordinary mind may ask questions such as, "Who is getting the cleaning now, you or the floor? Who is doing what?" From the sentient viewpoint, cleaning happens. From the consensus reality viewpoint of parts, all you can say is something paradoxical such as everything is getting cleaned and everything is doing the cleaning! IT cleans ITSELF!

This broom is doing Not-Doing
with you and the floor!

In any case, if you push yourself to do something, you
identify with one part of the whole and go against other parts.
Then you feel resistance in your body. Many body symptoms
are connected with "doing," that is marginalizing the available
energy of not-doing. Let "not-doing" do the things you have to
do. You may become more unpredictable in all that you do,
but you will surely have more energy! Wait until you become
aware of the subtlest tendencies, then follow them when they
are present, and not-doing will do the rest.

Lucidity, which senses tendencies for signals before
they actually become signals, does not just save energy—it
is also preventive medicine. Lucidity is something like dental hygiene. Dental problems occur when you do not brush
your teeth, but it takes months for teeth to decay if you do
not keep them clean and brush every night.

The same is true about physical health in general.
Lucidity is preventive medicine. Developing a relationship
to sentient experience works on body problems at a cellular
level before the signals become manifest. Do things when
they are "asking" to be done. You work less that way and do
more Dreaming.

NONTEMPORAL AND NONLOCAL EXPERIENCE

In the consensus realm of the everyday world, time is
associated with the sequence of events. First you get up, and

then you eat breakfast. One thing happens first, another second, in a linear time sequence from past to present to future. The same holds true for the idea of space—one place is here, the other is there. Events are localizable and separable. You start here and can trace your steps going to there.

But in the nonconsensual realm, in Dreaming, in the sentient realm before something is registered in our memory or consciously recognized, our experience of time is not linear. Ideas and events are "entangled." That is why you cannot say for certain from a videotape of a couple's signals who did what first. If you looked at a tape of Amy and me talking about the plum, you could not tell whether my sentient experience of the plum came before or after she sent out some sweet signal about the plum. If I look at my broom, you cannot track or measure whether I looked at my broom first or whether it flirted with me to get that floor swept.

You can differentiate CR signals we send one another by looking at a videotape. You can see my responses to verbal signals Amy initiates and vice versa. While you can see a couple sending signals to one another, you cannot tell whose *sentient* experience at the root of those signals came first or second.

Because you cannot see sentient experience—except when it finally manifests as signals—you do not know *where* or *when* in space and time sentient experience originates. *Sentient experience is nonlocal and nontemporal. Nontemporal* means that everyday time cannot be associated with Dreaming. *Nonlocal* simply means there is no single locality for sentient experience. Space and time are no longer firm concepts in nonconsensus reality.

We cannot say whether the sentient experience of that plum was local, whether it was in Amy or me, whether it was her process or mine. In CR, you can talk about Amy's process or my process. However, from the sentient viewpoint, you must think in terms of "our" plum process. Even better, you are safest if you think of the universe's process. Still better is that the plum arises from nothingness, from a void.

From the NCR viewpoint, you can only speak of process happening. As soon as you can see it in CR, it has a time and locality. Sentient processes, however, are like quantum processes—they are all over, "entangled," and they are present at all times until observed in CR.

Since sentient experiences are nonlocal and nontemporal, you cannot say for sure *where* the sentient experiences that lie behind your CR behavior come from. Your psychology and personality have roots in the entire universe. You do not know where your mind is located. Your consciousness and awareness are not only located in your body. It is exciting and interesting to try and track the mind in terms of the brain, as brain specialists are trying to do. Yet I fear we shall never be able to track the mind, because it is a quantum experience: it is Dreaming; it is an aspect of the whole universe.

The nonlocal aspect of sentient experience probably explains why shamans and medicine people who move through the realm of NCR say they work on the atmosphere of an entire community. They go into trances, have visions, and feel their experiences belong to everyone.

I remember the Kenyan shamans who did a healing on us in the bush in Africa, telling us that their visions came from the children in the village.[41] This was one of the reasons they gave coins, candy, and lots of love to their children. By analogy, you would have to give or say something sweet to everything you notice, since that is where your powers and visions are located! This is one example of how sentient experiences are nonlocal and nontemporal. Sentient psychology is basic to Buddhism, Aboriginal science, shamanism, and quantum physics.[42]

---

[41] See my *The Shaman's Body: A New Shamanism for Health, Relationships and Community* (San Francisco: HarperCollins, 1994) for more details on this healing.

[42] See my *Quantum Mind*, chapter 18, in which I explain how these realms are connected in terms of the mathematics of physics and mythological structures of early religions.

Psychology and physics are usually formulated from the viewpoint of a given social reality. For example, in everyday reality I am a white man, I am wearing black clothes, you are so and so, you have a name, you live on a certain street or are homeless, and so forth. Most people consent that this is reality.

But not everyone entirely agrees with consensus reality. Shamans and spiritual leaders indicate that what others call (consensus) reality is an illusion. Carlos Castaneda's famous shaman, don Juan, said that people who only follow consensus reality are "phantoms," while "real people" follow Dreaming, follow sentient experiences. Teachers such as don Juan value Dreaming reality as much as they value everyday existence.

Working with CR signals, parts, and particles is useful in psychology and physics, but many events remain mysterious if we only talk about parts. For example, synchronicities cannot easily be broken up into parts. When synchronicities occur, was it I who first thought about you, or was it you who first thought about me? One of the reasons for the confusion is that the terms, "you" and "I" are CR concepts.

Just as CR terms such as "you" and "I" are only approximations of sentient experience, the concept of parts and particles falls apart in quantum physics as well. At the subatomic level, there is a well-known failure of the parts theory called "the Bell theorem." In this theorem (and in the related Alan Aspect experiments[43]) one subatomic particle was found to be linked to its twin regardless of where the two were in space or time. The interconnection between particles occurs regardless of where or when they might be.

In the same way, synchronicity connects objects such as you and me in Dreaming, in a sentient nonlocal realm. People in relationships are always connected, for better and also for worse! All things are interconnected—we just do not always notice the connections.

---

[43] See my *Quantum Mind*, chapter 18, for details on the Bell theorem and Aspect experiments.

There is a Hindu tale about interconnections in Dreaming. In the story, before an unborn child comes out of the womb, she cries out, "Oh Lord, let me not forget who I am." Five minutes after she comes out she cries, "Oh Lord, I have forgotten who I am." In other words, when you are lucid of Dreaming, you know your whole Self. Once you are focused on everyday reality, you tend to forget your interconnection with all things.

CONSCIOUSNESS AND LUCIDITY IN THERAPY

You need cognitive ability in the CR realm to succeed in most of today's educational systems, including the study of psychology. In the future, we will have to develop programs that stress sentient abilities as well as cognitive ones. A Western-oriented therapist is trained to know things; she learns many bits of information, reads books, talks about various subjects, and knows lots of "parts." When she works with somebody in therapy, she "works." She has learned to set boundaries and be different than her client.

Western therapy, like Western business, is based in great part on some measure of performance. Both therapist and client are expected to make progress, develop, heal, grow, and succeed. This is standard Western thinking. The inner critic for many Western people is a mainstream Western mind that says, "You don't know enough, you don't work enough, and your performance is insufficient."

But there is an another, perhaps more ancient goal. Instead of knowing parts, people, and facts, the interrelationship between parts, people, and facts is crucial. Take, for example, the Asian tea ceremony. There is a form, a particular etiquette to use when making and drinking tea. Once you learn how to make the tea, the focus is placed on becoming lucid, spending time with each detail, tasting the tea, drinking it, and perhaps even becoming it. The important thing is not the actual drinking of the tea, but the meditative attitude, the relationship between yourself and all the parts needed to make and drink the tea. The lucid lifestyle behind the tea ceremony is the point, not the tea.

The concepts of doing and not-doing are based on two very different principles; consciousness and lucidity. Doing, or its Western definition in terms of "work," requires force carried out over time and distance. Work is connected to consciousness of difference, parts, effort, and power.

Lucidity applied to a given task transforms work into spontaneous acts of "not-doing." In not-doing, a phase of "doing" prevails while you learn the form of the task (as in the tea ceremony). But the rest is sentience, a matter of lucidity. There is no work involved. Things happen. You are present. Work finally gets done, but it is not work, it is not-doing; there was little force and no "I" involved. Work happened!

Not-working is difficult to talk about, but you can feel it because it makes you happy! Luckily everyone has a sense of what I am saying. You may remember learning to ride a bicycle. After a while, you stopped thinking about the elements of riding, and riding the bicycle happened automatically, almost without effort. Riding becomes an automatic, sentient experience. The "little you" does not need to be present.

To learn to ride, you must first discover the bike. It is different from you. The little you needs to work to learn the elements of doing something. Effort is required at some point in the beginning, but the goal is enjoying the ride, not working.

In not-doing, instead of asking about your performance, about whether you succeeded or not at some task, the important question becomes, were you lucid? Work is tiring; it is full of parts. But in not-doing, everything participates in the work.

By analogy, ordinary therapy is work; helping others is tiring. There are many problems, parts and facts. There are two or more people; there is a therapist, clients, medicine, and the world of duality and boundaries. There is illness and cure, society and the individual, dreams and reality.

All this is important, but exhausting. Not-doing is more seamless. From the viewpoint of Dreaming, it is not clear who is the therapist and who is the client. There are just two people, and nature is the Zen master. You are both there to study what happens. Things happen. Relationship does things. You work on the other, but at the same time, the work is done on you. Suddenly, it is the relationship that is transforming, as if by itself, and, at the same time, you or the other changes. Whoever you see as a therapist is another face of yourself. All day long there is nothing to do but become lucid.

The same thing holds for working with groups. In not-doing, the facilitator is no longer facilitator but rather an awareness practitioner following nature, getting things done, being part of the cleaning up of unconsciousness. This can almost be an automatic task! It is as if the tools for getting things in order, like a broom, work without the facilitator doing anything!

There is nothing wrong with using your mind cognitively; we first learn and break everything into parts, knowing who is who and what is what. There are great advantages to analytical thinking. In fact, to learn to be an artist, bike rider, therapist, or group facilitator, you need to learn about paints, pedals, dreams, and diversity issues.

But at another point we need lucidity. Sentience breaks down the boundaries and in a way, things happen. Learning happens. If sentient experience leads, then, regardless of what you are doing, work is no longer simple work. You are doing nothing all day long; you are no longer working at painting, bicycling, therapy or group work—in fact, there is no longer a you. Nevertheless, you can still sweat and look busy.

In not-doing, you are not a householder, parent, meditator, therapist, businesswoman, or social activist. You are part of things happening, becoming lucid and conscious of primal forces. You find your own special style of doing not-doing. No one drinks the tea the same way. Nature makes us look different, even if we really are not.

INTERCONNECTIONS

After all that talk about not-doing, my cognitive mind arises again. It wants to summarize what I have learned about tea drinking and not-doing and apply it to psychology and group work. My mind is proud of the chart below! This makes me laugh because the chart was not produced by the little me. It happened. But the little me likes to take credit for things if they come out clearly and refuses any connection to things that do not come out clearly.

Consciousness (Western)	Lucidity (Eastern)
Knowing, Working, Effort Study of Performance	Sentience, Not-doing, Awareness of Form
Performance: Get Better	Sense and Follow
Question: Did things improve?	Question: What is noticed?
Parts: Facilitator, Client, Group, you, Me and Objects	Sense of the Whole Each is everything
Boundaries are important.	Tao of People and things happening
Insight = Consciousness	Lucidity and Consciousness

In the cognitive world of doing, there is a you and an I as well as many more parts. I need you or you need me. You must work and perform so things improve. You gain insight. In the world of not-doing, you follow nature, focus on awareness and interconnection. Lucidity arises. That is how to not-work at things.

 ## THINGS TO REMEMBER

1. A good cook changes his knife once a year because he cuts, while a mediocre cook has to change his every month because he hacks.
2. If sentient experience leads, then, regardless of what you are doing, work is no longer simply work. You are doing nothing all day long; you are no longer working at painting, bicycling, therapy, or group work—in fact, there is no longer a you. Nevertheless, you can still sweat and look busy.

SIX

Reflection,
Flirting, and Beeping

Once upon a time, I, Chuang Tsu, dreamed I was a
butterfly flying happily here and there, enjoying life
without knowing who I was.
Suddenly I woke up and I was indeed Chuang Tsu.
Did Chuang Tsu dream he was a butterfly, or did the
butterfly dream he was Chuang Tsu?[44]

Chuang Tsu wondered if he was a person or a butterfly.
Based on our learning thus far, we might say that he was
Chuang Tsu in consensus reality and a butterfly in dreamland.
In other words, in CR he is called a person, but in dreams at
night and during the day, he is a butterfly. In Dreaming, he is
the essence of that butterfly, perhaps its sense of freedom.

Chuang Tsu as a butterfly

---

[44] *Chuang Tsu*, 49.

In this chapter, we will explore the interactions between CR, dreamland, and Dreaming. Until now, you have probably thought of dream images and projections as split-off parts of yourself. In other words, your identity was the little you, the center around which all things congregate and are to be integrated.

As you train your awareness to notice the Dreaming, you become lucid of sentient experience and, like Chuang Tsu, may begin to identify with Dreaming, or the Big You, that is, all the parts Dreaming unfolds into in your dreams. From this new viewpoint, you get the impression that there is nothing to integrate into your old identity; there is only a growing awareness of the Big You.

When you are lucid and sentiently notice the perceptual flashes and flirts that attract your attention all day long, you begin to feel that you are the essence of the things you notice. The little you is no longer the center of everything—your center shifts to your relationship with what you perceive. From the viewpoint of Dreaming, "you" are a sort of flirting or love affair with the objects around you.

This sounds a bit like the end of psychology; it is, as far as it is about consciousness of parts. Personal development now amounts to increasing awareness of perception. Your new identity is based on discovering sentient and observable aspects of the Big You. In this new view, "you" become everything around you, all the processes in your environment.

All of this sounds so far out to the little you that you may want to test these ideas. If you want to experiment, recall the objects you put in your room, the objects you love to look at. Consider the possibility that you might be the things around you that you love most.

For example, there is an old copper teapot on my desk. I make tea with it. My little me notices the teapot and thinks it is nice to look at. My little me just likes that teapot and is not very interested in allowing itself to experience the teapot flirting with me. As far as the little me is concerned, I am Arny and the teapot is the teapot.

The Teapot

From the viewpoint of the Big Me, however, that teapot is as much a part of Arny as the person called Arny. The Big Me is deeply democratic, and both Arny and the teapot are equally important! That teapot is an aspect of my larger Self, sort of tarnished, friendly, getting old, just being there.

The Big Me

The little Arny is more hassled, under pressure, trying to be more polished and useful in the world! The Big Me is different. The concept I am calling the Big Me (Big You) appears in Zen's idea of the "Buddha Mind," which is often pictured in Zen literature as a circle whose center is everywhere and whose circumference is without limit. Buddha Mind, or the Big You, is open awareness.

BUDDHA MIND: The circle whose center is everywhere and circumference is without limit.

The method of 24-Hour Lucid Dreaming is for gaining access to this Buddha Mind. When you have access to your Buddha Mind, its momentary center is the subtle relationship to whatever is catching your attention in a given moment.

You can check this out for yourself. If you like, experiment with the possibility that you are anything that catches your attention just now. Take a moment to gaze around you, noticing what catches your attention. What attracts (or disturbs) you the most? Stay with your little you and its observations. Notice that the little you assumes that feelings about whatever it observes can be marginalized.

Now experiment with being the Big You. See the little you and the things catching its attention as all being potentially valuable. Can you feel how, in some way, you are what catches your attention? Can you intuit how you might be everything in the universe? Can you see the environment as an aspect of the larger Self? How does it feel? If you can do this, you are switching between the Buddha Mind, or Big Mind, and the everyday mind of the little you.

In Zen stories, the Buddha Mind is sometimes pictured as a mirror that does not contain images, but merely reflects them. In other words, the Buddha Mind is a reflective, lucid attitude, but it is not any single thing that it reflects. If I am in a lucid mood, I have a Buddha Mind and am neither the teapot, nor am I Arny. Rather, I am the relationship to the teapot and to anything else that catches my attention in the ongoing stream of experiences that move through me.

JUNG AND CHUANG TSU

In the story of the Chinese sage Chuang Tsu, who asked if he was the butterfly, the Buddha Mind consisted momentarily of clearly seeing the little Chuang Tsu and the butterfly as both separate and interrelated.

Perhaps Chuang Tsu's story reminds you of moments when you also pondered who you were. It reminds me of one of Jung's stories from his autobiography, *Memories*,

Dreams, and Reflections. When he was eight, C. G. Jung was sitting on a stone and wondered if he was Jung sitting on the stone or the stone on which little Jung was sitting? Jung never answered that question, but he said he was upset by it for years.

I forgot I even had such questions until I began restudying physics in order to write *Quantum Mind.* The mathematics of quantum physics confronted me with questions such as "Who am I? Who is the observer? Am I the person sitting on my chair working at my computer, or am I the chair, which is being sat upon?"

Can you feel the state of consciousness in which you would even ask such a question? Take a moment and experiment with the state of consciousness needed to ask, "Are you yourself or the chair or couch or earth on which you are now sitting or lying or standing?"

You normally think, "I am sitting on this chair, or I am here and I am looking at a flower." But this viewpoint is only one of your possible viewpoints. It is a CR viewpoint. If you felt and thought like an Aboriginal person and did not marginalize your sentient experience, you would realize that your chair has power and is flirting with you, or trying to get you to pay attention to it.

In a sentient state, you sense your weight, the quality of the ground, couch, or chair you are on, and the relationship between the chair and yourself. If I feel that I am the chair, then I can go further and see myself through the chair's eyes. Try that. See yourself through the eyes of your chair or couch! What does the chair or couch think about you? Experiment with seeing yourself through its eyes. You use your chair, but perhaps you have not related to it enough.

You can do this experiment in lucidity with anything that catches your attention. For example, if I focus on the flower that now catches my attention, my awareness switches from myself as the observer to the flower, and then to the flower as a living being, as an observer. As I become lucid, I begin to sense the Dreaming connecting me to that flower; I notice the tendency to be a flower. Now my identity lies between the flower and myself. I can see the flower and me as separate parts and simultaneously experience a melting of the parts. I see the flower. Suddenly and for moments, I can look at myself from the viewpoint of the flower!

This is definitely an unusual experience. When I think in terms of parts again, CR comes back into being and I am looking at a flower, which is no longer me.

From the most sentient viewpoint of nonconsensus reality, from the viewpoint of Dreaming, neither the flower nor I exist. Instead there is a field experience without parts. Yet the only way I can verbalize my sentient experience of this field is in terms of the parts that catch my attention. I can speak of the field around me as a "flower-me dreaming." There is no separateness, there is just that process of flower-me, without anyone being separate from it. The flower and I are immersed in flower-Dreaming together. The ground of all the parts of myself lies is this "flower-me-Dreaming."

Traditional CR psychology stays in the consensual world and says the flower is a projection. You are there, and I am here, and this flower becomes at best an aspect of the psychology of the little me. I am projecting the flower onto the flower. Jung's stone is a part of Jung and the butterfly is part of Chuang Tsu. From CR psychology, these people are noticing parts of themselves that are stonelike and butterfly-like. From this viewpoint, you can withdraw projections and become more "whole."

Withdrawing a projection means that I know I am flowerlike. But withdrawing a projection also negates the Dreaming, the flower's nonlocal powers. If you withdraw projections, the little you gains something. But if you are not careful, you marginalize the Dreaming and inadvertently injure the environment by ignoring it. You put it down by devaluing the Dreaming.

For example, I love flowers, but if I focus only on "my" flowerlike nature, I am in danger of ignoring the flower's shared and nonlocal power, which involves me and everything else as well. The Big You's sentient viewpoint is that all the objects and feelings that catch your attention are aspects of the field. Explaining deep, sentient experiences in terms of words to the CR parts of your mind is not easy. Pictures help, but experience itself is finally self-explanatory.

See the pictures below to think more about the flower as an all-pervading reality, and also about the flower as separate from me.

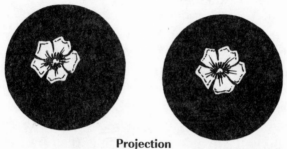

Projection

In flirting, there is reflection, you and the events which catch your attention overlap.

In CR states of consciousness, you marginalize the one-world reality, the flower-me world. "Reality" means the flower is not you. But early in the morning or in the NCR realm of sentient Dreaming, you, Chuang Tsu, Jung, and I are everything else we notice. You are the world, Dreaming. This is the Buddha Mind.

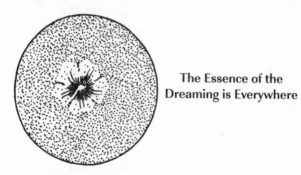

The Essence of the Dreaming is Everywhere

THE BUDDHA MIND IS LUCID OF FLOWER-ME DREAMING

Making the Transition between Realms

Let us now focus on exactly how we slip between states of mind, between everyday reality, dreamland, and Dreaming. To focus on these amazing transitions, I will go back to the analogy I spoke of in the first chapter, the analogy between the quantum wave function and Dreaming.

To make things simple, imagine the wave function for the moment as a sort of buzzing sound, not one that can be heard, but a barely audible buzz in the background of everyday reality. By analogy, Dreaming too is a kind of buzz. The Dreaming connected to the flower in our example is a sort of buzz.

Now, let us play with ideas. Let us pretend that everything you see is a sort of communicator and sends out buzzes, perhaps like a fax machine that buzzes others machines when it wants to send a fax.[45]

Let us say my flower is a kind of fax machine, and let us pretend that I am another fax machine. This unusual fantasy will help us understand how we flirt with one another, sending perceptual flashes back and forth.

Have you ever heard how one fax machine talks to another? Your fax machine (or the fax in your computer) calls your friend's machine and they beep at one another. The first fax machine buzzes "Beep, beep" to say, "Hello, are you there?" The other machine buzzes back, "Beep, beep, yes, I am here." This interchange is called an "electronic handshake." After this original handshake, which assures that both are tuned in to one another, the machines can communicate and send faxes to one another.

According to the physicist's interpretation of wave functions, and my understanding of the basis of quantum

---

[45] The idea for this example came to me from the imaginative work of Seattle physicist John G. Cramer, who attempted to give physicists an intuitive feel for what happens to wave functions in quantum mechanics during the process of observation. See the *Quantum Mind*, chapters 15 through 18, for more information on wave functions and how their reflection creates everyday observations.

physics, the flower and I are similar. In the NCR realm, we flirt with each other; we "beep and buzz" each other! You cannot see or hear these buzzes. They cannot be measured in CR; they can only be experienced.

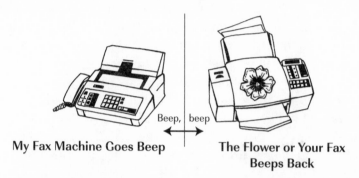

My Fax Machine Goes Beep

Beep, beep

The Flower or Your Fax Beeps Back

The picture on the left is meant to symbolize the essence of the flower in the world that "faxes" me, and the picture on the right is meant to symbolize the essence of the flower within me.

Once again, before the two machines can send faxes back and forth, that is, before they participate in what we might call a message exchange or an observation of one another, they must "shake hands." They beep to each other.

The beeping handshake is an analogy not only for what happens to computers and fax machines when they communicate with one another; it is not only an analogy of what happens at the quantum level in physics during the process of observation, but of what happens before observation between all objects!

Remember that Aboriginal Australians as well as teachers of the *Abhidhamma* speak of objects having powers to catch our attention before an everyday observation of these objects occurs! Remember how the *Abhidhamma* speaks about the earliest stages of perception? In chapter 4, I quoted Nyanaponika Thera's *Abhidhamma Studies,* in which he tells how bare attention notices these flashes or flirts that precede observation. In short, Aboriginal science, Buddhism, and modern physics all agree that an observation in CR requires beeps and handshakes in nonconsensual reality.

The flower beeps to catch my attention, to awaken me to its existence. After it catches my sentient attention, I am attracted to it and it begins to awaken part of me. Part of me sends back another beep that says, "I am here, let's communicate." In this type of communication, we cannot really prove who did what first, since time and space cannot be tracked in Dreaming. If this beeping is strong enough, the little me gets the impression in CR that "I" am looking at the flower and believes that "I" saw "it."

But when I am lucid, I no longer marginalize sentient events, and thus I notice the flower flirting with me even before I turn to look at it. I notice its power, its beeping in the nonconsensual realm. Then I notice something in me responding and beeping back, showing the flower that I got its beep. A reflection of beeps occurs in the nonconsensual realm between the flower and me.

When I am lucid, I cannot say that "I" notice and am doing these things. "I notice" is a common way of speaking in CR, but this way of speaking marginalizes the sentient experience of the flower-me field.

Thus far we have seen that Dreaming appears to the Buddha Mind or lucid attention as an underlying sense of unity and to the everyday mind as quick flashes and flirts between you and objects catching your attention that you will eventually observe. As you become more lucid, you can track the transition between Dreaming and everyday reality.

THE MYTHIC VIEWPOINT

This basic explanation of pre-observational experience is typical not only of quantum physics, Aboriginal Dreaming, and Buddhist science, but of myths from all over the world.[46] The fundamental concept of beeping back and forth, or of

---

[46] *Quantum Mind*, chapter 18.

mirroring and reflecting, which takes place in modern and ancient scientific understanding of the world, is found in native American traditions, in Chinese and Indian myths, in stories from Persia and Africa.

The sense that nature dreams Herself into being to look at Herself also appears in the mystical Jewish Kabbalah.[47] Myths from around the world speak of dreaming as the power of great universal beings that either created or are the Earth. Native peoples believed that when these beings dreamed, the world was created so the gods could look at themselves.[48] In all these stories, we find different versions of how a God or the Great Spirit created the world through Self-reflection.

A modern and playful rendition of this apparently universal principle is told by the American Taoist author Alan Watts in *The Book on the Taboo against Knowing Who You Are.*

God also likes to play hide-and-seek, but because there is nothing outside God, he has no one but himself to play with. But he gets over this difficulty by pretending that he is not himself. This is his way of hiding from himself. He pretends he is you and me and all the people in the world, all the animals, all the plants, all the rocks, and all the stars. In this way he has strange and wonderful adventures, some of which are terrible and frightening. But these are just like bad dreams, for when he wakes up they will disappear.

Now when God plays hide-and-seek and pretends that he is you and me, he does it so well that it takes him a long

---

[47] The reason for the everyday world is that "God wished to behold God." According to the Kabbalah, before the universe began, "There was a previous non-existence in which, as the written tradition says, 'Face did not gaze upon Face.' In an act of total free will, God withdrew the Absolute All . . . to allow a void to appear in which the mirror of existence could be manifested. . . . God's place is the world, but the world is not God's place." I found this mystical passage in the otherwise easily read book, Z'ev ben Shimon Hilevi, *Kabbalah, Tradition of Hidden Knowledge* (London: Thames and Hudson, 1979).

[48] In my *The Year I* (London: Penguin-Arkana, 1990), I speak about the relationship of these myths to world problems.

time to remember where and how he hid himself. But that is the whole fun of it—just what he wanted to do. He does not want to find himself too quickly, for that would spoil the game. That is why it is so difficult for you and me to find out that we are God in disguise, pretending not to be himself. But when the game has gone on long enough, all of us will wake up, stop pretending, and remember that we are all one single Self—the God who is all that there is and who lives forever and ever.[49]

Anthropos myths and Watts's story carry a similar message that everyday reality is a manifestation of Dreaming, that is, of tendencies reflecting on themselves.[50] Everyday reality is not the deity itself, but a manifestation of the Dreaming. By remembering your ability to do 24-Hour Lucid Dreaming, it is possible to remember the Big You.

The concepts of mirroring and the reflection of flirts are central not only to mysticism, Aboriginal traditions, and Buddhist science, but also to the mathematics of physics. Without such mirroring, the present theory of quantum physics and its explanation for reality could not exist.

MARGINALIZATION

When you are not lucid, you marginalize flickering flirts and flash experiences to the outskirts of your focus. These experiences seem to have no meaning, seem too quick or vague to be important. You may be able to catch yourself marginalizing Dreaming in the morning, when you tend to pay more attention to what you must do today than to that irrational sleeping and awakening experience.

---

[49] This quote comes from the Vintage Edition of Alan Watts, *The Book, or the Taboo against Knowing Who You Are* (New York: Vintage 1972), 14.

[50] Anthropos myths see the universe as a humanlike being. When this being goes to pieces, as in the case of Ymir, a Germanic Anthropos figure, the world and its parts come into being. The rivers come from its blood, the trees from its hair, and so forth.

Marginalization is not just "bad"; it is a part of nature. For example, you have certain things to do during the day. You feel tired upon awakening; sometimes you need to marginalize that fatigue in order to do those things. Conversely, if you marginalize your experiences too much, they become symptoms. Marginalization does not destroy events—it simply places them outside of your awareness.

From the viewpoint of 24-Hour Lucid Dreaming, from the viewpoint of the Buddha Mind, with bare attention you will notice that the apparently separate people and objects, plants, and animals of the everyday world are not only separate. This field is permeated by the Dreaming, in which each object flirts with the others in a massive, entangled unity.

Native traditions speak of all events as part of a family. Everything together participates in creating reality, and the trees, rocks, the sun and moon, are all our sisters and brothers. From an NCR viewpoint, the everyday world is a huge, semi-human field of relationships, of flirts and flashes!

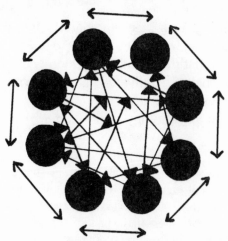

The Sentient Field in Back of Consensus Reality

The diagram above, which shows the flirts and flashes between the objects of everyday reality, reminds me of a group of dreamers, perhaps a group of sheep, sleeping and dreaming together. When the dreaming field awakens itself, so to speak, the group "disentangles" itself and the world becomes a group of separable individuals and objects.[51]

From the viewpoint of Dreaming, when the world awakens, sentient experiences unfold and create the CR realm of duality. Because you marginalize the Dreaming, the world only seems to disentangle the overlapping, you-me-flower oneness in back of CR. In principle however, and with lucidity, you may notice that entanglement still remains in the background. You think things get clearer and separate, but that is only because you focus on their separateness and marginalize the entanglement.[52]

You could say that as the Dreaming field begins to awaken, it reflects on itself. It unfolds into separate parts and each part, one after another, marginalizes the background and thinks the other is flirting and trying to catch its attention. In that moment of reflection, separation becomes possible and the world of parts, including the observer and the observed, is created.

What terms can we use for this process? The terms depend on where you are coming from. Myths speak of great deities awakening from their slumber. A physicist might say the field of unbroken wholeness begins to unfold itself. A meditator might say that the Buddha Mind looks in a clear mirror.

I suggest that the universe has its own spontaneous awareness process that awakens to itself. If we review the facts of physics, psychology, and meditation, the traditions

---

[51] Physicists study only the CR realm and think that the observer disentangles the sentient background of reality by deciding to observe. The physicist's idea that the observer disentangles through wanting to observe places consciousness in the hands of an "observer." According to this idea, the act of observation "collapses the wave function." The term "collapse," means that the wave function, the mathematical analogy of Dreamtime, loses its imaginary character upon self-reflection. Before such reflection occurs, the piece of matter described by the wave function can be—as in Dreaming—anyplace, anytime. See my *Quantum Mind*, chapters 14 through 18 for more.

[52] See footnote 46 for more on this point.

of Aboriginal cultures and shamanism, it appears that the tendency toward self-reflection and consciousness is a natural law. When Dreaming reflects upon itself, we have everyday life. Why this happens is a matter of personal belief. Regardless of the belief we hold, it seems that life itself results from a symmetry principle, to Self-reflection.

From the viewpoint of bare attention and Dreaming, you awaken conscious because the world wants to reflect on itself and create parts, one of which is called you and another of which is called me. In other words, from the Dreaming viewpoint, no one does anything; lucidity and consciousness just happen. In the thinking of shamanism, Buddhism, and Aboriginal traditions, humans do not play a central role in creating the world; the world is created by everything because of its sentient nature.

EXPERIMENT IN UNFOLDING

From the Dreaming viewpoint, objects and people are equal. No one thing is more central than any other object. Each time you observe something, it has interacted with you in part because of its power. In the following inner-work experiment, you can explore the sentient power of objects.

The early alchemists from Africa, China, Europe, and elsewhere saw matter as possessing a soul. They spoke of an object's inner power and ability to catch your attention as the object's soul or "*Ignis Innaturalis*" (meaning "a hidden, immeasurable fire"). This natural fire was needed for transformation to take place. The alchemists meditated on this fire, putting the object with its own *ignis* in the pot to focus on. Because of the *ignis*, the object transformed. [53]

The *ignis* is another term for the flirt, the Buddhist *dhamma*, the root, spark, soul, and generator of life. Now I

---

[53] See Carl Jung, "Psychology and Alchemy," *Collected Works*, vol.12 (Princeton, N.J.: Princeton University Press, 1969); also see my *River's Way: The Process Science of the Dreambody* (London: Penguin, 1985) for more on the "*Ignis Innaturalis*."

would like to give you time to experiment with nature, its flirts, and its *ignis*.

In this exercise, I suggest that you use your awareness and pay attention to flirting. This requires extending your attention to irrational happenings. You will notice and focus on things that you normally marginalize. Hold them in your focus and watch them cook.

To expand your attention in the following exercise, I will suggest that you allow your everyday mind to relax, to be "clouded." This idea comes from Lao Tsu, who says in the *Tao Te Ching*, "I alone am clouded, everyone else is clear." Being clouded allows your lucid ability to work. Cloudedness will avoid your habitual tendency to make meaning out of events before they have fully appeared to you.

Part I: Everyday Mind and Dreaming

We should first ask your everyday mind to give us permission to explore Dreaming.[54] Is doing such an exploration okay with you? You might want to know that nothing is going to happen that is not already happening in some way to you. To begin, get into a reasonably comfortable position and concentrate on yourself.

First, let us invite your everyday mind to formulate questions you may have had about your life. What has been puzzling you in recent times? Write down one of your central questions.

Now, if your mind allows itself to relax, take a minute and encourage yourself to let go. Become clouded, if you can. Let your everyday mind become foggy, unknowing, and empty. Try closing your eyes and focusing on your breathing for a few minutes. If you still want to keep track of reading this book, just leave one of your fingers on the spot where you were last reading.

---

[54] If you choose to do this experiment with another person, the helper simply focuses on awareness. Ask the other, again and again, "What are you experiencing? Have you marginalized anything?"

When you feel you are ready, begin to slowly open your eyes. Half open them and slowly gaze around. Let your Dreaming mind notice what things flirt with you. If several things catch your attention, let your Dreaming mind choose one of them to focus on. Use your attention to catch this flirt and hold it.

Be patient and loving: notice and stay with what caught your attention. Just be with it. Use your bare attention; hold your focus on it even if it seems meaningless.

Part II: Shapeshifting

Now, see if you can sense the essence of the object that caught your attention, its root or basic tendency or quality. This may be an irrational feeling, but just feel that. Next, experiment with letting that quality unfold. In other words, let it elaborate on itself. Follow its energy, its *ignis*, and its power to unfold. This may be incomprehensible at first. Do not worry about that. Just hold your attention to the power of that object and watch it unfold itself in terms of feelings, images, and sounds.

When you are ready, experiment with letting the essence of this visualization have a human form or voice. See it, hear it. This may be very irrational. Encourage yourself to let a face appear.

Now try being this visualization; let your human form change shapes, that is, shapeshift. Feel that face, see it, be it. Step into its nature, its mind.

When you are ready, look at yourself through its eyes and see your little self looking back at it. Stay in the imaginary realm. Check out if you feel you are it or if you are marginalizing it. How does the ordinary you look in its eyes? Have a chat with that little you, if you can.

Let the essence of this visualization express itself using your hands. Let your hand movements express its essence. Give it time. Let it describe itself with your hand motion, or let it draw itself or create music, poetry, or anything else. Take time here. Let it speak words; write some of them down.

Part III: Divination

Now it is time to think about meaning, and to slowly come back to your everyday life. To begin, ask yourself the following questions: How, when and why do you marginalize or tend to marginalize this aspect of yourself? How do you put this Dreaming to the edge of your awareness? When do you do this? Consider keeping this experience more central in your life.

Look at the basic question you wrote down in the first step of this exercise, the question your everyday mind had about your life. How does the proceeding experience and face answer that question?

What does the experience of this flirt mean for your everyday life?

Finally, see if you can allow yourself, in your present mood, to consider the following: what does the everyday little you mean for the event that flirted with you?

It is possible that the sentient essence of the thing that caught your attention has always been a crucial part of who you are. Explore and feel the sentient essence of the object that flirted with you and experience how it is trying to realize itself in your life. Enjoy and play with the idea that the Big You is a combination of your everyday face and the face of the object that flirted with you.

Remember the answers to your questions, and above all, remember that face and the Dreaming power behind the object that caught your attention.

In this experiment, you may have discovered the commonness connecting you to the things that flirt with you. In the past, you may have thought you were attracted to or fell in love with your opposite. That is correct from the CR viewpoint. But from the sentient viewpoint, you are not attracted to your opposite. Rather, you are constantly falling in love with yourself.

 ### THINGS TO REMEMBER

From the viewpoint of sentient experience, you are having a love affair with the objects around you.

Dreaming appears to the Buddha Mind as an underlying sense of unity. To the everyday mind, Dreaming first appears as quick flashes and flirts between you and objects catching your attention.

When Dreaming flirts and reflects upon itself, everyday life appears. Why Dreaming does this is a matter of belief. Regardless of what that belief is, it seems that life itself results from a symmetry principle, Self-reflection. Dreaming is the source of reality.

From the sentient viewpoint, you are not attracted to your opposites. Rather, you're constantly falling in love with yourself.

SEVEN

Theory and Practice of Divination

How do I know the ways of all things at the Beginning? By what is within me.[55]

To be in contact with what is going to appear next in life, you need to be lucid about what is within you, about sentient experience. If you notice your deepest Dreaming and the flirts that unfold from it, you become a diviner, sensing the hidden future.

Becoming lucid of sentient experience is more than putting the little you aside and submitting or discovering something that is greater than you are. The method of 24-Hour Lucid Dreaming is a lifestyle change in which your ordinary identity relaxes and transforms in order to form a relationship with the field in which you are living. As the above quote from the mythic Chinese sage Lao Tsu indicates, this transformation is the basis of Taoism.

The Taoist follows that which has not yet unfolded, "the Tao that cannot be spoken." This attitude does not have strict

---

[55] Lao Tsu, in *Chuang Tsu*, 127.

programs, dogma, or rituals associated with it. Revealing the future is a by-product rather than a goal of that attitude. The legendary founder and first identified Indian historian of yoga, the second century B.C. mystic, Patanjali, emphasized that states such as telepathy and clairvoyance were not the aim of yoga practice; they are by-products of this practice. Yoga is meant to suppress the contents of the mind.[56]

THE THEORY OF DIVINATION

How does the divinatorial "by-product" of lucidity come about? Though divination and prayer are as old as humankind, little is known about them. Divination is closely connected with lucidity, shamanism, parapsychological powers, and synchronicity. While we will not be going into detail on the topic of divination, I would like to point the interested reader to fascinating studies of this topic by psychologists C. G. Jung, Charles Tart, and Henry Reed, to mention but a few researchers.[57]

---

[56] *Cittavrttinirodha* ("the holding or stopping of the mind stuff") was how he described it. Patanjali's model of mysticism comes from the *Mandukya Upanisad*: "The Fourth [aspect of self], say the wise, . . . is not the knowledge of the senses, nor is it relative knowledge, nor yet inferential knowledge. Beyond the senses, beyond the understanding, beyond all expression is The Fourth. It is pure unitary consciousness wherein [all] awareness of the world and of multiplicity is completely obliterated. It is ineffable peace. It is the supreme good. It is One without a second. It is the Self." From *The Upanishads, Breath of the Eternal,* trans. by Swami Prabhavananda and Frederick Manchester (Vedanta Press and Bookshop, 1996).

[57] See Jung's seminal work "Synchronicity: An Acausal Connecting Principle," in volume 8 of his *Collected Works*. Charles Tart, a psychology professor at the University of California at Davis and longtime researcher of psychic phenomena, has done many fascinating experiments with his students. See Professor Henry Reed's informative description of Tart's work in *Awakening Your Psychic Powers* (New York: St. Martin's Press, 1996), 6. Reed's solid study of the medium Edgar Cayce's "paranormal" abilities includes an interesting bibliography for those readers wanting to know more about this subject.

For any theory of divination to be accepted, it must be able to account for this practice's ability to predict and explain events. Furthermore, it must be consistent with other theories such as psychology, physics, Taoism, Aboriginal science, and Buddhism. Finally, it should lead to a practice that can be taught. The exercise at the end of this chapter will give you the chance to learn and test the theory created in this chapter.

Interestingly enough, a divination theory may include invisible elements such as the Tao or Dreaming. There are many things in life we accept without understanding because they seem self-evident to us. For example, we do not understand gravity, or love, yet both explain something about how objects and people come together. In the latter part of the twentieth century, physics has developed new ideas such as "virtual particles" that cannot be experimentally checked, but that give rise to results that can be checked.[58]

No one has ever seen virtual particles. They do not exist in the consensual sense of little objects you can locate. No one can prove that they exist; yet people talk about virtual particles because the theory is consistent with other acceptable concepts and theories.

Any theory of divination must be simple, evident, and easy to grasp. Einstein said that the simpler a theory is, the better it is. Theories that are too complicated are not believed, and a theory that is too complicated cannot easily be checked against our experience.[59]

---

[58] Physicists think of virtual particles as bumping and banging into one another to explain the attraction and repulsion we associate with electric and magnetic fields. Many hope virtual particles will explain gravity fields as well. According to particle theory, electric repulsion no longer results from an electric field but from the virtual particles that create the field. See my *Quantum Mind* for more.

[59] For example, I was not convinced of quantum theory before I could prove for myself that its formula matched psychological experience.

PATTERNS OF DIVINATION

A theory of divination should apply to various kinds of diviners and to the fact that divination has been used since the beginning of time the world over.[60] John Mathews's wonderfully illustrated text, *The World Atlas of Divination*, inspired me to envision the first diviners as cave people. Can you see people standing in a cave in front of a fire, looking into it and having visions?

Thousands of years later I see a shaman sitting at a riverside, or standing at a mountaintop. I see him singing or whistling and falling into trance-like states. In these states he divines the answers to questions. See the picture below.

Shaman Opening up to the Wind and Sky

Still thousands of years later, I see a woman in a shawl sitting in front of a crystal ball. Can you see her too? Somebody is sitting on the other side of her and asking, "How many children should my daughter-in-law have?"

The cave person, shaman, and crystal ball gazer are all diviners. While the cave person and village shaman use their lucid attention to sentiently experience and divine the future,

---

[60] Divination and shamanistic systems evolved from the Celts, Europeans, Jews, Greeks, Africans, and Native Americans and from the Arctic and Eurasia, China, Tibet, Australia, New Zealand, and India. Today in the West, many new systems have arisen.

the crystal ball gazer is more closely connected to the interpretation of Dreaming that has unfolded in terms of the wind
in the trees, the patterns dry bones make on the ground, the
motions of the stars, and the patterns of tea leaves.

All diviners go through phases of lucidity, ecstasy, and
interpretation. The more ecstatic diviners go further into
their dreaming to find new information, while great interpretive diviners stay in consensus reality and interpret acts of
fate. One of my clients even uses his TV. When he no longer
knows what to do with his life, he turns on the TV and tells
me that the TV shows him where he is at in that moment.

You can use any flirtlike, chance event in interpretive
divination, as long as it has an uncontrollable aspect. Coins,
dreams, the cracks in turtle shells, the lines on your palms,
the motion of a pendulum, the stars, cards, sheep, apple
peelings, coffee remains, the TV—all will do.

Any beginning theory of divination must include the
Dreaming realm in order to be consistent with Aboriginal science, psychology, physics and Taoism and to include the different types of diviners. Various diviners either sense the
Dreaming directly, notice flirts that unfold from the Dreaming,
or are adept at interpreting flirtlike and uncontrollable phenomena such as the throw of dice or other acts of chance.

Dreaming is the reason a diviner knows things about
you from a distance and throughout time. Dreaming is nonlocal and nontemporal and relates to everything in your
everyday reality. The Dreaming is called by many names: the
Tao in Taoism, tendencies in quantum physics, sentience in
psychology. Later on, we will see how Dreaming can also be
felt in your subtlest movements.

Divination procedures differ only in form. In Taoism,
you meditate and let sentient experience unfold by flipping
coins a number of times to produce an answer. In physics,
the Dreaming is analogous to the quantum wave potential,
that is, to tendencies that Self-reflect to produce the proba-
bility of certain events occurring in everyday reality. Using
movement, you can let sentient experience unfold by
sensing subtle movements and following spontaneous

motions. These tendencies are the basis of predicting the future of a given situation; they are reflected in the mathematics of physics to create probabilistic answers.

The basic idea in Taoism, physics, and movement work (as we will soon see) is that sentient experience unfolds and explains itself. You have already experienced in the last chapter how sentient experience reflects on itself, allowing you to shapeshift into new experiences that provide answers to unanswered questions.

Related aspects of divination found in the Dreaming of Aboriginal science, in Taoism, movement work, and physics can be seen in the diagram below. You will notice a certain consistency in the various areas, that is, each area manifests the same pattern in which a self-amplifying sentient experience unfolds into an objective result.

DIVINATION METHODS

Physics	Movement	Taoism	Dreaming
Tendency	Sentience	Unsaid Tao	Dreaming
Quantum Flirt	Sense Subtle Motion	Meditate on The Moment	Become Lucid
Self-Reflect	Self-Reflect On Movement	Coin Flip Flip again	Self-Reflect Shapeshift
CR Observation	Dance-story	Hexagram	Vision
Consensus Reality	Story	Answer	Insight

THEORY OF DIVINATION

Cloudedness:

Divination procedures begin in nonconsensual realms, in Dreaming, where your everyday mind is relaxed. This is why divination experiences may begin with some procedure that allows the everyday mind to become clouded, and why the great mystic sage, Lao Tsu, says in the *Tao Te Ching*, "I alone am clouded, everyone else is clear." To begin with, you need to accept foggy states, relaxing, not knowing what to do. Cloudedness and relaxed focus are important attitudes in all divination procedures.

Shapeshifting:

Ecstatic diviners practice some form of "shapeshifting," which means allowing yourself to experience the figures, times, and spaces of your dreamland and Dreaming experience. In shapeshifting, shamans "shift" their experience from their human shape into the dreamland figures they are experiencing. Shamans may use drugs, drumming, dance, or fasting to create and reduce ordinary consciousness, allowing shapeshifting to occur.

This Shaman Shapeshifted into her Spirit Form

Shapeshifting is one of the shaman's great powers, which allows her to leave the human realm and identify with the world of animals and spirits. Shapeshifting involves letting go of your human form and becoming the sensation, object, demon, or animal that you have seen in a vision. Acting out a figure from one of your dreams in an authentic manner, truly feeling and moving like that figure, is a method of shapeshifting.

MOVEMENT DIVINATION

Now let us experiment with divination by using your spontaneous movements to find answers to questions you have about life. In the following experiment, you shall begin by asking a question, and then follow your spontaneous body movements to find the answer.

In this process of divination, you will be able to practice certain feeling skills or "metaskills." [61] *Relaxing your ordinary mind will be helpful in exploring the Dreaming. If you remain clouded, you will eventually be able to sense the Dreaming and its self-generating properties. If you would like an example of this kind of work before you begin doing it, read the note at the end of this chapter.*

Although you can do the following movement divination process in a sitting or even lying position, I suggest standing or at least sitting on the edge of your couch or bed, since these postures are most helpful in understanding the nature of your body.

1. *The Question.* Make yourself comfortable sitting or standing. Focus on your breathing for a moment. While you are relaxing, ask yourself a question that you might ask a diviner. What question about your life would you like to have answered? Write down your question.

2. *Cloudedness.* From your present position, preferably sitting or standing, relax and try to let your ordinary mind become clouded. With a gentle focus, notice or catch the subtle motions your body tends to make even *before* they occur.

   Experiment with feeling and opening up to these tendencies without knowing where they will lead you. Focus on the tendencies without yet following them. Allow yourself to explore and be unknowing about these subtle, sentient experiences. Your exploration may be a bit irrational, as slight tendencies are often incomprehensible at first. If you feel this way, you are on the right track. Just persevere. Let your ordinary mind be patient, and use your lucidity to track your experience as it arises.

---

[61] See Amy Mindell's *Metaskills: The Spiritual Art of Therapy* (Tempe, Ariz.: New Falcon Press, 1994).

3. *Lucid Attention.* Be clouded and unknowing about what these motions want to do. Use your lucid attention to Dreaming to catch and be open to these tendencies.

Now, begin to follow these tendencies by moving slightly in the direction the subtle movement wants you to. Reflect that motion, that is, follow it. Give these movements space to unfold, let them generate and unfold their own movement story. Perhaps irrational visual images appear, or memories and stories. Let the movement and visual processes unfold, even if you do not know where they are going.

4. *Shapeshift.* Next, experiment with shapeshifting. Notice the movement and imagery and, when you are ready, step out of your ordinary identity and allow yourself to become the figures or sensations that are now appearing to you. This may be new for you, and it may help to pretend that you are an explorer getting to know your total self.

Now that you are this movement, it can generate its own meaning! It will explain itself. Just remain lucid as the Dreaming unfolds into Dreamland images and stories. Give it time.

5. *Meaning.* Stay with this experience a couple of minutes. Perhaps it will generate something meaningful connected with the question you asked in the beginning. Explore how your experience connects to the question you originally asked. Ponder the answer. Appreciate the answer. Consider how to apply it—what it means for your various relationships, your connection to the world.

6. *Healing.* Which part of your body did that movement work? Think about your body—your knees, hips, back, your neck, head, and ankles. Think about your posture, energy, skin and blood pressure. Did that movement work focus on one part of your body, on an area with any aches, pains, or problems?

Perhaps the movement process you experienced was healing some aspect of your body. Consider how this movement process is trying to bring your attention to a particular posture or part of your body that has been flirting with you without your realizing it. Find answers, enjoy them, but remember the cloudedness, the dreaming process that brought you here. The great danger is that we will marginalize the experiences that brought us answers.

If you stick to answers and marginalize the sentient experience, your life will become a series of questions and momentary answers. However, if you avoid marginalizing the sentient processes, your life will be based on change, the Dreaming itself.

Telepathy and clairvoyance are not the aim but the by-products of yoga practice. Remember Patanjali's wisdom quoted earlier (see footnote number 57 on page 99). "Beyond the senses, beyond the understanding, beyond all expression is The Fourth. It is pure unitary consciousness wherein [all] awareness of the world and of multiplicity is completely obliterated. It is ineffable peace. It is the supreme good. It is One without a second. It is the Self."

The divination *process* is the key to life. The answer you get is only a momentary solution to one specific question. Sticking to the answer and forgetting the process would be like remembering what you learned and forgetting God.

This point reminds me of Mother Cabrini, a clairvoyant Italian saint who lived in the early twentieth century. She could see into the hearts of others, find water, and do many other such things because of a power she called "Jesus." She never allowed anyone to call her the founder of the Missionary Sisters of the Sacred Heart. She always said that Jesus, or Mother Mary, Mother of Grace, had founded the institute. As to the many charitable establishments she created, she remarked, "I have done nothing. The sacred heart of Jesus has done everything. I am merely a witness of the wonders of God." When someone spoke of her humility, she gently replied, "Humility, I am a poor nothing, capable of doing nothing but evil and ruining God's work."[62] In other words, even more than the answer or results you get, the divination experience of Dreaming is itself the key to a complete life.

 ## THINGS TO REMEMBER

A divination theory should be consistent with Aboriginal science, psychology, physics, and Taoism and also includes the different types of diviners.

This theory is: divination comes from becoming lucid about sentient or quantum realm events that unfold into everyday reality.

Not the answer, but the divination *process* is a key to a complete life.

ENDNOTE: A DIVINATION EXAMPLE

The following example comes from work I did on myself while writing this book.

After meditating on what question wants to be answered, I realized that my question was, "What is the best attitude for me to work on this book?" Sometimes I am very excited and work all night, while at other times I get very tired. Should I push or just follow my energy?

Cloudedness. The first step for divining an answer is to become unknowing about my own movement. To do that I must feel it and relax, allow myself to "not know" what it is that my body wants to do.

Since I want to do a movement-oriented divination, I stand for a few moments and just sense my body and the subtlest movements. This is a bit disorienting, because I do not know what is going to come up.

---

[62] Timothy Conway, *Women of Power and Grace, Nine Astonishing, Inspiring Luminaries of Our Time* (Santa Barbara, Calif.: The Wake Up Press, 1994) 46-47.

I begin by watching how my movement evolves from this standing position. I notice that I feel a little shy doing this and reporting on it in a book. Now I am relaxing, and I feel myself getting clouded. After a minute or two, I begin to notice a tiny "something" in my knee. It almost feels like my knees want to give way, to buckle under me. Becoming lucid for me means noticing this subtle flirt, a movement sense of "giving way." I will give it a chance to express itself by reflecting it, letting it amplify itself.

I notice my body beginning to lean backward . . . now I am feeling as if I am falling backward. Suddenly I am in the middle of a Dreaming, an imaginary process of some sort. It is unfolding itself. At first I have no words to describe my sensations, then I find myself in a vision, twirling backward in space, going backward and backward.

I notice that I am no longer my ordinary self; instead I have the sense of my shape shifting. Though my real body is still standing, leaning slightly backward with my feet placed firmly on the ground, my dreaming body is twirling in the air.

While I am twirling, my ordinary mind is beginning to return. It is wondering about this experience, wanting to know its meaning. Since the meaning is not yet clear, my cognitive mind will have to be patient while my process continues to unfold. In my experience, I am still twirling backward in space . . . twirling. . . . Suddenly, I see my twirling body becoming a wheel . . . and I am suspended in space just outside or off the wheel.

I got it! I just got the answer!

Now I can say it in words. I experienced myself twirling backward, spiraling in space. Suddenly, I saw my twirling self turn into a wheel! At first, that wheel seemed so irrational I thought, "Forget this, it is too strange to be possible!" I was the wheel or bound to the wheel, but then it spun me off into space. Now I am sitting outside the wheel looking at the world.

Then I got it!

Then I got it!
ATTACHMENT AND DETACHMENT.

My process is giving me the feeling of detachment. Do you remember my original question about how to write this book? The meaning that my movement experience generated for me is, "Be the wheel, get on it, get attached, and through attachment you will get off the wheel and detach. Do not be afraid of being attached and trying hard. Through that, you will detach."

Now I have the answer from my movement divination. The answer is, "You need to be on the wheel and uptight, then you will get off the wheel." The divination procedure told me that, through living my worldly ambition, I will be able to detach from it. As I continued writing this book, that attachment and detachment process was exactly what happened.

II. Lucid Healing

Time Travel

You are born in a human form, and you find joy in it.
Yet there are ten thousand other forms endlessly
transforming that are equally good, and the joy in
these is untold.
The sage dwells among those things, which can never
be lost, and so he lives forever.
He willingly accepts early death, old age, the beginning
and the end, and serves as an example for everyone.[63]

The proverbial sage is definitely more detached than
most of us. She is born into a human form in a consensus
reality, but shapeshifts throughout life and death. In this
way, she models for others how to live forever by being like
the spirit of transformation itself.

In this chapter, through the study of the patterns of
quantum physics, shamanism, and Taoism, we will explore
leaving the human form and traveling backward and forward in time into past and future lives. Normally, you may
feel that time and space are crucial and that the past is

---

[63] *Chuang Tsu*, 123.

something that cannot be changed. Sometimes you may feel programmed and impinged upon by time. Hopefully, this chapter will change your feelings about history and time.

Before launching into time travel, let us review what we have been discovering up to this point. In part one, we focused mainly on the theory and practice of 24-Hour Lucid Dreaming and its connections with Aboriginal wisdom, Buddhism, physics, and divination.

Based on our discussion thus far, we must consider that:

- Dreaming is the oldest human form of spirituality; it is central to many Aboriginal cultures and is a basic pattern behind Taoism, Buddhism, and quantum theory.

- Without access to Dreaming, you may feel that something is missing in life; you focus only on the moon's bright side and ignore its totality.

- Dreaming appears at first as a vague tendency or premonition of things to come; Dreaming is a presignal experience. Dreaming reflects and self-amplifies in the form of communication flirts to create the observable forms we see in everyday reality. Likewise, the mathematics of quantum theory predict that observable reality arises from Self-reflecting quantum wave functions.

- "I" do not perceive, but am part of a Self-reflection process with the universe around me. "I" do not observe, but am first attracted by objects that have their own power to "flirt" with me.

- My normal identity is the result of marginalizing the larger part of myself, the Big Me, which includes everything that catches my attention.

- In Dreaming, consensus reality concepts such as I, you, me, and she are vague and entangled processes that cannot be easily differentiated.

There are at least three ways to become lucid of Dreaming experiences.

- You can sense sentient experience before it manifests in everyday reality.

- You can notice flickering signals and events, such as sudden thoughts or a momentary body feeling, to find their sentient essence.

- You can become lucid by focusing on signals and sensations that persist, such as body symptoms, by guiding yourself back to the "roots" of these experiences.

Part two of this book is devoted to training your focus in these three aspects of lucidity. In this part, we will explore the applications of lucid dreaming to various aspects of life, such as stepping out of time, and to dealing with body symptoms, addictions, body contact, relationship issues, and large group problems.

STEPPING OUT OF TIME

If you have ever experienced a déjà vu, or sensed that you were transported—with or without drugs—into another time and space, you will understand Chuang Tsu, quoted in the beginning of this chapter: "You are born in a human form, and you find joy in it. Yet there are ten thousand other forms endlessly transforming that are equally good, and the joy in these is untold."

Many people feel they have been someone else, or have lived in earlier times. Most people have had some form of this time-shifting experience at one point in their lives.

Space Ship
Leaving the Earth's
Time and Space

When I ask my classes how they think time displacement occurs, they bring forward a number of theories, including:

- Stepping out of time and space comes from the Spirit. I am just a vehicle for what happens.

- There is no time. Whatever reality we step out of or into is really happening all the time.

- Ancestral memory accounts for time displacement experiences. We experience something that was experienced by our ancestors and carried forward, or given by them. Time displacement can be thought of as "soul memory" triggered by sight, sound, or smell, as experiencing something the soul has experienced in another body, in another lifetime.

- Déjà vu occurs because of the power of certain highly magnetic or condensed areas of the Earth.

- Time displacement is a body experience that happens, for example, when several people in a room simultaneously have the same memory of another time and space.

FEYNMAN'S THEORY

These theories reflect the mystical and parapsychological ideas of various traditions. It may be surprising to some readers to discover that the pattern for time displacement can be found in quantum physics as well.

For example, Nobel Prize-winning physicist Richard Feynman developed his own theory of time travel to describe the behavior of elementary particles, though he never called their behavior time travel. He suggested that the mathematics of elementary particles in quantum physics described the world in two different ways: going forward in time, and going backward in time. By studying and interpreting quantum physics, he discovered that two separate realities were possible, one of which physicists had not yet discovered, which is the reality of going backward in time.

His theories gave me the general patterns to connect the psychology of altered states with the behavior of particles in quantum physics.[64] If you have science anxiety, do not panic, and do not worry about the physics! I use Feynman's theories as metaphors for psychological theories. You can take his theories as something like a dream that offers you a new pattern for exploring the universe.

Feynman studied the formula for elementary particles such as electrons. He knew these formulas predicted known experimental results, but he also thought that the formula predicted new and undiscovered electron behavior when electrons entered a magnetic field.

As you can imagine, whenever a charged particle such as an electron enters an electric field, it gets pushed and pulled around, much as tiny pieces of metal might get pushed around in a magnetic field.

Feynman gave two interpretations of how this pushing and pulling occurred. One of the interpretations involves the spontaneous creation of "virtual," short-lived particles. They exist so briefly in time that you will never be able to measure them. The second interpretation does not involve virtual particles, but the possibility of traveling backward in time, or out of time.

According to Feynman's first interpretation, when an electron enters into an electric field, virtual particles are

---

[64] For more details, see my *Quantum Mind*.

suddenly and temporarily created. These virtual particles bang into the original electron that is entering the field, deflecting and changing its direction. This may sound strange to the reader unfamiliar with physics, and indeed virtual particles are strange. Although they cannot be seen directly, their possible existence is allowed by the theories of modern science.[65]

The physics may be more understandable to you if you think of a social analogy in human life. Do you remember the first time you had to speak in public? As soon as you even thought about the room where you were to speak, all sorts of inner figures popped up in your head. Some wanted to help, while others criticized you. These figures do not exist in reality, but they have an influence on your state of mind.

Feynman's first interpretation of what happens to an electron in an electric field is similar to a human being who enters into a speaking field. Positive and negative virtual particles appear out of nowhere to change the original electron's course. In this interpretation of quantum events, an electron entering a magnetic field is banged by a particle with an opposite charge (a positron) that knocks it out and sends the original electron in new directions.

In a second interpretation, Feynman looked at the equations of physics and realized that another interpretation was possible. Instead of virtual particles, the electron entering the field could *move out of time* and experience "time travel" or even go backward in time for a split second. After that split second, it could go forward in time once again, reemerging from the field, moving in a new direction.

In brief, the first interpretation involves virtual particles that give the electron a bang, but no backward movement in time. The second involves a backward time movement, but no virtual particles.

Both interpretations are allowed by the equations of physics because no one can say for sure exactly what happens when an electron enters an electric field. We cannot

---

[65] See chapters 33 and 34 in my *Quantum Mind*.

directly measure things that happen so quickly. All we can do is measure overall results; we cannot track little particles because of a basic uncertainty in nature. Since both theories are consistent with the rest of physics, they are acceptable, possible theories (awaiting new experiments and theories that explain things even better).

In the diagrams below, I have portrayed Feynman's question and two different answers about what happens to the original electron entering the field.

These diagrams are called "space-time diagrams." The horizontal line represents movements in space, while a vertical line moving upward represents time, which goes forward. All events that move forward in time will be heading upward on the page.

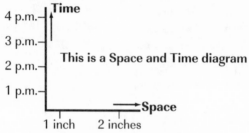

THE FIRST DIAGRAMS:
WHAT HAPPENS IN A MAGNETIC FIELD?

Feynman asked, "What happens to an electron when it enters a magnetic field?"

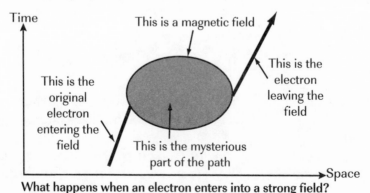

What happens when an electron enters into a strong field?

To answer his own question, Feynman drew a diagram like the following:

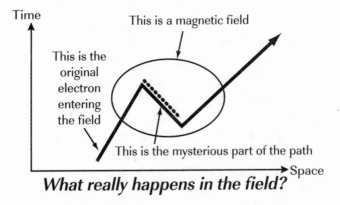

What really happens in the field?

After drawing the diagram, "What really happens in the field," Feynman proposed two possible explanations to how the field affected the electron. Let us call the first the "bump theory" and the second the "backward movement in time theory."

FEYNMAN'S TWO ANSWERS

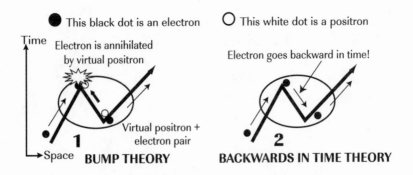

These diagrams may look weird, but actually they are not much different from a picture of marbles hitting one another.

In diagram one to the left, the bump theory, the original electron entering the field is annihilated at the top of the diagram by a positron (which was a member of the virtual particle pair created earlier in time).[66] In the diagram to the right, the backward in time theory, there are no virtual particles—instead the electron itself meets the field and reverses itself and goes *backward* in time.

This second diagram indicates the big surprise. *When an electron meets a field, it may go back one minute or ten thousand years in time*, depending on the situation. (Since we cannot measure what has happened, it might even have gone into the future first!)

Today, no one can check for sure which diagram is right; physicists imagine that the electron simply has both possibilities—or else simply view the second scene as interesting but experimentally unverifiable.

FEELING INTO THESE DIAGRAMS

Now, to understand how you can move backward, or out of the forward march of time, you need to get a feeling for what is happening in these diagrams. Let us begin with diagram one.

If that electron were sentient and could speak like a human being about to give her first speech, when it entered the room it might say, "Hmm, something tense is happening here. I don't want to pay attention to that tension now but will focus on the speech I am about to give. I will try to keep going and ignore the tense field in this room."

This electron does not experience the field lucidly; instead it marginalizes the magnetic field and tries to continue

---

[66] In the diagram on page 120, a virtual particle pair is created to the right of the entering electron and one particle of this pair annihilates the original particle while the other virtual particle becomes real and leaves the field. (The virtual pair is composed of a positron that annihilates the original electron, and a second electron that leaves the field.) A positron is an antimatter version of an electron; it is exactly the same except its charge is positive instead of negative. According to physics, the virtual pair is created by small fluctuations in energy. For more about virtual particles, see my *Quantum Mind*.

on its way. At first it gets confused, tense, almost knocked out by that tension. Inside its head it meets a critical voice and gets so knocked that it cannot remember its speech. This electron is annihilated, so to speak. If I continue to anthropomorphize the path of that electron, I can say that it was not lucid about the field; rather it marginalized it. After a while, it recovers after forgetting its lines, goes on with the speech, and feels better.

Now let us look at diagram two. Let us pretend again that the electron is not only sentient, but lucid. Since the electron is lucid, it moves into the tense magnetic field and feels it. If the electron is a person, she notices at this point that things are getting weird in the lecture room. Some unknown tendency is at hand. Instead of marginalizing this tense experience, she decides to become lucid and relaxes the way she was going.

She becomes clouded and gets to the core of the field, she senses something critical. She experiences criticalness and a critical inner figure. Now, instead of going forward, she steps out of time, becomes this critical figure, and begins to tell the audience that she has always been critical of what she is going to say next. She goes back in time to when her own critical power began to develop and takes the whole audience backward in time with her. They are surprised, yet very interested by her humility. She is speaking to something in each of them.

Finally, she completes her brief review of her earlier life and tells people that her critical nature has helped her be careful about everything she says, and to not hurt others but to remember everyone. After saying that, she notices the field changing and experiences herself coming back to the way things were before this critical field was there. As she comes back to the present moment in time, she begins to give the lecture she had planned.

After "retroflecting" on the past, she comes back to everyday reality and continues to move forward in time! Her tensions are gone, and her lecture proceeds wonderfully. "Friends," she says, "now that I have shown one side of myself and perhaps of the field around our topic for the day, I would like to present the other side, the topic itself!"

No one, inside or out, annihilates her or even thinks of criticizing her; she has incorporated all possible thoughts into her own path. She is everyone and everything.

Feynman's two diagrams describe approximately what the electron might experience. Of course, he did not speak about sentient or lucid beings. He simply gave two basic mathematical patterns for these two different allowable phenomena.

Everyone has had personal experiences that can be mapped out by these diagrams. Each time you enter into a tense field, or an exciting situation, you act out either the Bump or the Backward in Time Theory. If you are not lucid, you marginalize the tension and are moved about by positive or negative inner figures. Conversely, if you are lucid and follow your inner experience, you leave your self-definition behind. Shamans have always done this by shapeshifting, stepping out of time into new forms and times, and later reentering the "real" world with new information from the "other world."

Analogously to the Feynman diagrams, there are two kinds of psychology. In one, you live your life and develop secondary processes, that is, if something bothers you, and you feel it is not part of who you are or want to be, you ignore it. That is the story of the "edge." The ignored event does not go away, but it eventually disturbs your attention or even knocks you out. Most of us behave this way most of the time. We move into troublesome spaces and exceptional periods of life and insist on pushing forward, refusing to let go of our identity. Then we somehow get bumped.

The other possibility is that we move out of time and space and let go of our identity. We become lucid about our sentient experience and, even before it manifests positive or negative figures, we become edgeless. Even before we can talk about a tension, we change and let go of our hold on time and go with the flow. Such moments require a lot of awareness, personal courage, and flexibility.

For example, when I was a psychology student in Zurich in the 1960s, I saw a therapist, Franz Ricklin, a nephew of C. G. Jung. Weird things always happened around him. I once made an appointment to see him on Saturday. When it was time for my appointment, I went into the old part of Zurich where his office was located. It was a lovely fall afternoon, the trees were colorful, and the bells of Zurich seemed to be ringing joyously.

But Ricklin did not come to the door after I rang for several moments. I thought something unusual was happening. I rang and rang and, after getting no response, patiently sat and waited to see what would happen next. About five or ten minutes went by and, without wanting to, I apparently fell asleep sitting on the ground, leaning up against the front door of his office.

About an hour went by before his door suddenly opened, as if by itself. In a sleepy trance, I fell over, pouring onto the floor of his waiting room. I looked up and saw him standing there above me, rubbing his eyes, looking groggy himself. Apparently he was just waking up as well!

Wobbling on his feet, he said in a sleepy voice, "What's happening?" I said in an embarrassed and irritated tone, "You didn't come at the right time!" He countered, equally irritated, "This *is* the right time, *now*." I said defensively, "Right time for whom?" He roared with laughter until tears poured from his eyes as he pronounced mysteriously, "Right time for us."

I had no idea what he was talking about. My mind was distracted by a sudden fantasy. I could not go further into that conflict because I suddenly saw spirits flying through his room. Though I was shy about this vision, I told him about the spirits. He said calmly, "Stay with that. What year is this?" I thought I was going to lose my mind. This was not the kind of therapy I thought I needed, but I said that it felt like we were in the fifteenth century. Off we went on a fantasy trip into the fifteenth century. He was ready for anything, and I was too, at least around him. Around certain powerful people it seems easy to step out of time. Around other people, you cannot get into a trance even if a stone bangs you on the head.

Ricklin always moved in other times and spaces. That afternoon, my relationship to him gave me the courage not only to sense the groggy, sleepy field we were in, but also to take that field as an opportunity and golden chance to step out of time.

TIME TRAVEL EXERCISE

Time travel events occur spontaneously, or you can train yourself to experience them whenever you want to. This training is the goal of the next exercise.

To do this exercise you will have to give yourself permission to imagine once again that your form can change. You will be experimenting with your fate. (If for some reason, you are shy about altered states of consciousness, just read this exercise; you need not immerse yourself in it.)

FLIRTS IN REALITY

Describe your ordinary life, your present experience of time and space.[67] What is life like? Is your time cramped, boring, relaxed? What is space like for you? Do you experience it as full, empty, colorful, infinite, confined?

Relax, once again; assume an attitude of not knowing, of cloudedness. Close your eyes and focus on your breathing. Notice the nature of the field around you, the kind of psychic or physical atmosphere in which you are now living. This is like the magnetic field influencing the course of the electron. Is the field tense, weird, or is it enjoyable?

Use your lucid attention. If you are meditating, slowly open your eyes halfway, and with half-closed eyelids, gaze

---

[67] If you do this exercise with someone else, focus on being an awareness facilitator. Simply note if and when the dreamer is reflecting or marginalizing her experiences.

around. Let the field express itself in terms of something that catches your attention. If several things catch your attention, let your unconscious mind decide which to focus on.

Find the essence of the thing that catches your attention, and explore the energy or power of this essence. Be patient; explore its sentient core, the seed from which this object came.

Stay in the world of this essence, of prematerial events, of dreaming. This requires lucid attention. Do not marginalize your experience because it seems too irrational. Just let it arise in connection with your attention. Do not let yourself be diverted. Describe the world of this essence, the thing that caught your attention. Explore its time, its space, and its atmosphere. What is time like here? What is space like?

Step out of ordinary time. Imagine the time period and spatial location, the world from which this event came. When you are ready, let go of your definition of yourself and experiment with changing form. Shapeshift. Let yourself step out of human time and be in the new time and space of that object. Feel and then step into its time, its sense, and then move in its space. Imagine moving, feeling, seeing, living your new self. Be there if you can. Shapeshift.

Step out of time and describe this new life. Do you have a particular role in that world? Take time with this experience. Imagine a story about the experience of your role in this period, let a story unfold, let there be music, poetry, and art. This takes relaxation and trust in your fantasy. Let yourself dream. Finally, let this experience rename you. What is your true name? Take time in this, let it influence you now today.

From the viewpoint of this new world, look at yourself in ordinary time. *How do you look in everyday life?* Is there anything about the life you had while time traveling that you would like to bring into your ordinary life?

Consider your two lives—what do they share, what is similar? This similarity is a something you may want to be more aware of. This commonness may be the timeless, immortal part of you.

Notice if and when you marginalize this eternal part of yourself. Note or feel what kind of life this new aspect of you is trying to generate.

Consider one of your problems, tensions, or conflicts in everyday life. How is it connected, if at all, with marginalizing your eternal self?

The field you are living in expressed itself in terms of your time travel, a sort of virtual reality, just as the critical lecture hall created critical figures in the mind of the lecturer. Analogously, the electric field created virtual particles that banged into the electron.

Instead of being bumped by virtual experiences, you stepped into them and into another time period by being lucid of what catches your attention. Shapeshifting, feeling yourself into what is happening, and letting go of your ordinary self, you stepped out of time. This exercise is training in what the shaman don Juan calls, "controlled abandon," following a path of heart, the sentient path. It is as Chuang Tsu has said, "You are born in a human form, and you find joy in it. Yet there are ten thousand other forms endlessly transforming that are equally good, and the joy in these is untold. The sage dwells among those things, which can never be lost, and so he lives forever."[68]

By dwelling among timeless experiences that can never be lost, you discover that aspect of yourself that lives forever.

 ## THINGS TO REMEMBER

Feynman's theory of what happens to an electron in an electric field is a metaphor for what happens to you because of a given atmosphere.

In one scenario, you get bumped and fused.

In another, you become lucid and shapeshift, stepping out of time into an eternal part of yourself.

---

[68] *Chuang Tsu*, 123.

NINE

Lucid Healing, Preventive Medicine

The hundred joints, nine openings, and six organs all function together. Which part do you prefer? Do you like them all equally, or do you have a favorite? Are they not all helpers? Can they keep order among themselves, or do they take turns being leaders and helpers? It may be that there is indeed a true leader. Whether I really feel his existence or not has nothing to do with the way it is.[69]

Who is the body's leader referred to by Chuang Tsu? When I began investigating symptoms in the 1970s in Switzerland, I had no idea who this leader might be. I only knew that the body is led by Dreaming. Let me tell you how I arrived at this thought. When I first experimented with symptoms, I discovered that every body symptom or pain

---

[69] I have quoted this from *Chuang Tsu*, 25, but I changed the translation found in that book by substituting the word "leader" for "master," and "helper" for "servant," because I feel that these words better reflect the feeling and language Chuang Tsu meant for today.

could be found reflected in the images of dreams. I called this reflection the "dreambody."[70]

For example, one of my clients described his headache as a bomb that was about ready to explode. When I asked him what he dreamed the night before, he said that he had dreamed about an explosion! This is a typical example of how uncontrolled body experiences are mirrored in dreams. Reformulated, you might say that your body is dreaming. When focused on and amplified, body experiences always appear to be reflected in dreams you had before the symptoms appeared.

The picture below shows the body dreaming—this man is suffering from a headache and dreaming of an explosion.

The Dreaming Process

The Physical Body

The figure on the left is nervous and has a headache that feels like his head is exploding. This experience is pictured in a dream. The physical headache and the dream of an explosion are the body and dream aspects of the dreambody.

THE DREAMBODY

After working with thousands of people on their dreams and body symptoms, I can draw several conclusions:

The concept of illness is part of the medical paradigm, which sees symptoms pathologically.

---

[70] See my *Dreambody*.

As far as your personal experience is concerned, every symptom is an expression of Dreaming and can be seen in dreams.

Symptoms are therefore part of your overall development and awareness process.

Scary body symptoms are like "Big Dreams"; they carry important, dramatic information about life.

Anyone, whether child or adult, has an opportunity to transform a painful and terrifying symptom into an enriching life experience by shapeshifting into the Dreaming behind symptoms.

Like all signals, body symptoms have unfolded from Dreaming, sentient experiences.

Symptoms are keys to enlightenment. They teach you about your chemical and physical body (do not drink black coffee if you have an ulcer), your dreams (that is, your explosiveness) and with lucidity training, your Dreaming.

As we move through this chapter, we will learn how to train ourselves to discover this Dreaming before symptoms actually become symptoms. In fact, becoming lucid about sentient experience might reduce or even be the cure for some symptoms that are difficult to feel. In my experience, lucidity may reduce the prevalence and lethal power of diseases such as multiple sclerosis.

Since the sentient experience of a symptom manifests physically in the body, the Feynman diagrams, which describe patterns behind physical observables such as an electron's direction, must also describe body symptoms. You may remember that whether or not an electron (or other particle) becomes annihilated or steps out of time depends in part on "its" lucidity.

Since you are composed of the same kind of energy and stardust as electrons, the laws of physics will be true for you as well. Extrapolating from physics into psychology means that if you are lucid about sentient experience, you have at least two choices as to how you experience a symptom. You can experience symptoms either as self-annihilating or as an invitation to step out of time.

In the same manner as our time-travel experience, I will show that when you relax your identity and follow your sentient experience, a symptom will take you out of your ordinary self and into the realm of ever-changing identities. The less you marginalize body experience, the less troublesome body symptoms appear.

For example, I know someone who has been working on herself a long time. She has suffered from multiple sclerosis, a chronic disease affecting many nervous system functions. When I first met her, she had a bit of trouble keeping her balance while walking and felt weak and unstable. At first she tried to allow her symptom's message into her life and allowed her life to become unstable. She freed herself from many things as a first step toward "integrating" the signals of the disease.

Integrating signals into everyday life is like integrating dream experiences. This physical and psychological work can be relieving. For example, as this woman worked on herself for several months, she became more lucid of her sentient experiences and was able to sense the onset of symptoms hours before they actually occurred.

Her lucidity of sentient experience allowed her to become more fluid and make changes, to step out of linear time before her symptoms "annihilated her," that is, before they actually manifested as symptoms. She told me that she could feel fatigue "knocking at her door" in the subtlest way, encouraging her to relax and do something more restful instead of pushing forward thereby avoiding symptoms before they manifested.

The more you marginalize the sentient origin of symptoms, the more you must deal with symptoms in a mechanical way. Then, when symptoms bother you, you try to eradicate them with painkillers. Without sentience, or the ability to process the dreaming behind your symptoms, you tend to be like a dentist or a body mechanic, surgically removing or drilling to remove anything you feel does not belong.

The psychological or spiritual way of dealing with symptoms is based on the paradigm that what is happening is an ultimate mystery that we can only follow. The medical paradigm is more mechanical. The picture on page 132 shows the medical or mechanical way of dealing with body symptoms—get rid of them at all costs!

Standard Method of Dealing with Symptoms

In the conventional medical paradigm of pathology, you treat your symptom as something that is wrong. Your body is like a machine or an inanimate object; if something is wrong, you fix it mechanically. From the experiential viewpoint, however, symptoms indicate that Dreaming is appearing in the body. Symptoms are not only hell. They are powerful signals, big dreams trying to happen, and your job is to experience that big dream as soon as possible.[71]

Review of Dreambody Work Methods

Before discussing how to work lucidly on symptoms, let me briefly condense and review symptom work from the process-oriented viewpoint.[72] Then you will be able to better understand exactly where lucid symptom work fits in.

---

[71] To find out more about how to work with symptoms, see my *Working with the Dreaming Body* (London: Penguin-Arkana, 1984).

[72] Process-oriented symptom work is based on the idea that a physical symptom is not only a medical problem, something to be cured, but rather a potentially meaningful and physical expression of the Dreaming, much as dreams are essentially visual expressions of the Dreaming. By exploring the nature of the symptom, the process-oriented therapist hopes that new parts of an individual's life will open up, and also, that the symptom will become less important, or even disappear.

There are at least six different possible methods to consider. Each method is connected to a particular aspect of symptoms. Which method you apply depends on your ability and the situation.

Symptoms are connected with dreams. Hence, simply understanding the dream can be helpful in relieving the symptom. For example, understanding and experiencing the dream of the explosion can relieve a headache.

Besides being connected with dreams, *symptoms are connected with internal physical sensations.* Getting the message of these sensations is relieving. For example, take that explosive headache. The "explosion" is what you might feel if you put your hand on your head. You feel the pounding sensation of the headache as the blood bangs up against the arteries, veins, and capillaries.

Then instead of focusing only on the headache and the need for an aspirin, you would focus on exploding, expressing yourself emotionally about something. You might make exploding, angry sounds, hit a punching bag, or play drums. Such work often relieves symptoms.

Angry, Explosive Expression

Symptoms are connected to relationships. In the first cartoon of the man with the headache on page 129, you see him tapping his fingers on the table. This tapping is a body signal that occurs when he is nervous, or unaware of his pounding explosiveness. Such signals may appear when he is alone or in relationship to someone else.

If I were sitting with him and saw his tapping on the table, I might ask him to explore what that signal is expressing. When amplified, that tapping might transform into knocking and he might discover and then say that he was impatient with me. The basic idea is that the symptom's energy appears not only in dreams or in his headache but in communication signals such as the tapping finger as well.

The multidimensional way in which symptoms manifest is the reason that body work and dream work are not sufficient; signal awareness must also be learned to bring out the Dreaming (or symptom's) messages into relationships. Symptoms return when relationship signals are ignored. Symptom work is a kind of relationship work that proceeds by bringing the symptom's power into everyday communication. For example, thinking about the headache again, that man might focus on using the symptom's powerful energy in relationship by being more impatient, or more dramatic.

These first three methods are useful for symptoms that are so strong (or have "very great" power, to use a term from the *Abhidhamma*) that they easily reach your everyday awareness. The next three methods are useful in working with subtler, less easily felt symptoms, or as preventative symptom work.

Subtle experiences of the back contain dreamlike information. As my work with the dreambody progressed, I extended dreambody work by focusing on eliciting subtler experiences such as those that occurred, for example, while touching the back. If someone moves their hands over your back, pressing gently as they move, you will become aware of experiences, or pressure points, you may not have felt before.

Working with these otherwise unfelt experiences, amplifying the sensations and letting them unfold in fantasy and movement, brings forward areas of awareness that are usually deeply unconscious. This method is useful in working with body problems whose origins cannot be normally felt. Without knowing it, I had found a physical method of accessing sentient, subtle, and as yet, unmanifest body experience.[73]

For example, by pressing on a certain area, a point, you might have the sense that a piercing needle is sticking into you. By feeling and imagining further, the point that feels like a needle might turn out to be clear and piercingly powerful ideas you have, clarity that you are shy about expressing.

I began to incorporate methods I learned from the Egyptian Book of the Dead into body work. These methods incorporate the attitude of worshipping and speaking directly to the soul of the body. In this irrational method, one person relaxes or lies down, and without touching the person, another person speaks directly to different parts of the body, calling out to them, so to speak. This method elicits deep body experiences as well.

If you would like to try this, lay down and ask a friend to address a part of your body that is bothering you. Let her say to your body, focusing, for example, on your stomach, "Dear stomach, know that we are listening to you, and that we honor your messages. Please feel free to manifest in the form of a body feeling or images or words." You can be sure that your stomach will have a lot to say. Try it, and notice the resulting experience.

Sentient Body Work

Now let us move on to explore the sixth method, lucid, or sentient, symptom work. Sentient body work finds and works with the essence or root of the symptom. Let us go back to the example of the man with the headache. In sentient symptom work he would feel the blood going through his head and might feel the blood knocking or pressing

---

[73] Dr. Aminah Raheem of Santa Cruz, California, has elaborated on this method and connected it with acupressure, developing a method she calls Process Acupressure. See her book *Process Acupressure* (Palm Beach Gardens, Fla.: Upledger Institute, 1996).

against his cramped arteries.

Then, instead of only focusing on that knocking signal or unfolding it in terms of pounding or drumming, he would imagine going beneath that explosive sensation to its root, to the sentient essence of the symptom, to its existence as a tendency before it became a signal.

What is the sentient, presignal experience that preceded that explosive, dramatic headache? The sentient essence behind the explosiveness might have been a sense of power. The symptom itself, explosiveness, was preceded by a sentient sense of power, which was marginalized, ignored, not noticed. When feeling powerful is marginalized in the sentient realm, then the signals of the headache arise and finally appear in anger.

Working at the more overt level with the signal of anger is interesting and important psychological work. But it differs from working sentiently, which is more preventative. Sentient body work deals with the quantum level of experience, so to speak. Remember Feynman's electron and positron, or reversal in time? In one of those quantum processes, you experience signals (such as criticism) annihilating you. In another process, you become lucid about sentient experience even before a symptom manifests and annihilates you (and become self-critical, as in the example in the previous chapter).

Sentient symptom work is similar. When you feel the symptom coming, you focus and live its Dreaming. In the case of the headache, this might mean feeling a headache coming on and living close to the sense of inner power. It is difficult to verbalize lucid or sentient symptom work because the experiences involved are an aspect of Dreaming that is difficult to formulate. Soon we shall be doing an experiment where you can experience such work yourself.

In what follows, you will be stepping into your body processes and energies *before* a symptom appears and becomes annihilating or agonizing. The important questions will be, "What was the symptom before it was a symptom? What is its tendency or root?" You will then apply your lucidity to step out of time and go into the timeless and spaceless world of Dreaming. You will be asked to shapeshift, letting yourself transform into other figures.

These six different methods are summarized below.

Symptom Work	Method
1. Symptoms in Dreams	Understand dream
2. Symptoms as the Body Dreaming	Feel, amplify symptom, compare experience to dream images
3. From Relationship Signals to Symptom Work	Notice signal, connect with symptom. Or bring out symptom energy as a signal in relationships.
4. Sensations arising out of Back Massage	Notice back experience, amplify and unfold into story
5. Symptoms accessed through speaking to them (Egyptian method)	Acknowledge and call to symptom in the body to express itself.
6. Lucid or Sentient Body Work	Discover the origin of problem before it is manifested as symptom.

SENTIENT SYMPTOM EXERCISE

Choose a body symptom to focus on, preferably one you can feel. If you have no symptoms in the moment, reexamine a symptom you once had and want to know more about. Choose just one.

Now begin to focus on the symptom. Do not focus on the effect the symptom has on you, but on the element that seems to create the symptom. For example, if you work with a headache, do not just describe the effect on you, namely, that it makes you tired, but try to describe the element that creates the headache pain itself. Then you might sense an explosiveness that seems to create the headache.

Even if you have meditated or worked a lot on yourself, you may find resistance to focusing on the origin of the symptom. Be patient with yourself. It is normal to want to marginalize something that bothers you. Marginalization is not helpful, however, so feel the symptom and try to experience what seems to be creating it. Try to re-feel that symptom so exactly that you could actually re-create it or describe it so well that another person could almost feel it if they wanted to.

Now unfold that description. For example, if you feel a weakness, concentrate and follow that sensation. Imagine that weakness, feel it. If you feel pressure, go ahead and image some sort of pressure maker. If you have a sharp pain, let that sharpness unfold itself, see it as a knife, for example. If you sense something growing within you, let the growing something pictorialize itself in your mind. Perhaps you will see that growth as a plant. Use your own body sensations and let them create images.

The images that describe your body sensations are parts of your dreamland, your psychology. Your body creates dreams. But we do not want to stop here. We want to go deeper into the origin of the symptom, before it even became a symptom.

Sense the sentient essence of the flirting symptom. Find the roots of the symptom experience, its essence, the very origin of the symptom experience before it became a symptom. Imagine the sentient essence behind the symptom, the tendency that it was before it became a symptom.

To find the sentient experience, search for the first tendencies that occur before your symptom even became a symptom. Feel the symptom and go backward, get to the essence at the base of the symptom before it appeared. Take your time doing this.

For example, perhaps a sense of protectiveness or motherliness came before a symptom that feels sharp because that sharpness was a reaction against something bothering you. You needed protection. Or perhaps the essence of a symptom of pressure is a sense of freedom that became a huge pressure pushing outward when freedom was impinged upon. The sentient essence is very elementary. Use your own meditative awareness to explore the sentient root of your symptom.

Now focus on this essence, using your lucid attention; study this sentient Dreaming that is the deepest core of that symptom. What is this world like? What are the time and space of this world? Instead of marginalizing this Dreaming experience, let your identity go. Feel yourself into this sentient world. Living in its time and space, be there, stay there. What is the nature of the times and spaces of protectiveness, freedom, sensitivity, power, or whatever you are experiencing as the essence?

Be lucid and shapeshift into the times and spaces of that symptom's sentient essence. Notice if you are marginalizing the experience. Try to be generous and consider the possibility that the everyday world is no more or less significant than the world you are exploring. Try taking both worlds as equally important. Try living in the space and time of the sentient essence of your symptom.

Unfold this essence. What sort of life does this sentient experience tend to generate? What pictures unfold from it, what parts? Can you see images? Paint, portray this world in music. Let the atmosphere amplify itself in Dreaming. Experiment with this sentient essence, using movement, drama, stories, or any method the essence calls for. Stay in this drama, this art, this being.

Consider the possibility that you yourself are living art, being dreamed and created. Take time to be this sentient experience. Let its world create life! When you live in the world of this essence, notice how your sense of time and space changes. Is there something in you that tends to marginalize this experience? Why do you marginalize it? What would it take to stop marginalizing?

Consider how these experiences might influence you in your daily life. How do they influence you now? Consider using these experiences in your work. What about your life, your attitudes, and your behavior might have to change?

Now that you are this essence, feel or know what is needed to care for your body, to relieve your symptom.

This exercise is a type of lucid dreaming. By tapping the

tendencies and source of symptoms before they manifest, the work you have done is a kind of preventive medicine. Such "medicine" is a lifestyle change in which you take time to notice sentient experience and let it create life.

THE CLAMP THAT WAS A FLOWER

The method of 24-Hour Lucid Dreaming with body symptoms requires training, mindfulness, and concentration. But anyone can learn it. I remember a participant in one of our European symptom seminars who had no previous training in psychology or meditation. She complained about a pain in her upper back that did not respond to medical or alternative medical treatments. Whatever she did, that pain remained.

When Amy and I asked her what that pain felt like, she said it felt like a cramp. Her image of that cramp was something like a metal clamp which, when screwed tight, would not let go. Hearing about that clamp, we naturally asked her about what she had let go of, thinking that the clamp was there for a reason. Sure enough, she told us that she wanted to be strong and independent and did not like to "hold on," even when an intimate partner of hers said he was leaving. She told us that she refused to hold on and preferred to just let him go. With some encouragement, we suggested that holding on (like a clamp) might be useful, and she cried, saying she did not want to hold on and be emotional. But as soon as she cried about his leaving, she already felt better.

So far we had been working in dreamland with her. She had felt her symptom, described its image as a clamp, and realized that although she did not like holding on, she needed to, at least to the point where she could discover and express her feelings about things.

Then came the lucid body work. When we invited her to tell us what that clamp was before it was a clamp she had a hard time understanding. Amy suggested that she feel the clamp, and go back to its beginning, to its origins, to the time when it was only a tendency. What sort of tendency was that clamp? To the participant's surprise, she herself found that the sentient essence of that clamp was a flower! She said that before her body "clamped up," even before she refused to show emotions or hold on to a relationship that was breaking up, the clamp was a flower.

Flowers, the Clamp's Essence

In other words, before she clamped up, the tendency in the background was to be exquisitely sensitive, like a flower. The flower was the root of the clamp. She explained to us that whenever the flower was ignored (marginalized), when its extreme sensitivity went unseen and unfelt, her body cramped up.

Amy and I invited her to shapeshift and to live for a while in the world of that flower, its time and space, its fragrance, and sensitivity. She loved that flower-Dreaming. Then we suggested she remain in contact with that flower-Dreaming even while she was in relationship with others. We acted out different relationship issues in her life. To our surprise, she was able to remain in the world of that sensitive flower and to relate to people as a flower might. Depending on the situation, she "drooped," "wilted," or "bloomed."

Knowing yourself means knowing the Dreaming from which symptoms arise. In that world, there is less pressure from human or social behavior; you are closer to nature, to existence as it is. Lucidity changes your life. Knowing the Dreaming behind your body and its symptoms can affect you; it works on your "illnesses" and psychology without really working on them.

 THINGS TO REMEMBER

Symptoms are a route to enlightenment. They awaken you to the mystery creating your life as well as new aspects of your body's chemistry and psychology you might otherwise never consider.

Lucidity might reduce the prevalence of diseases such as multiple sclerosis.

The central question is: "What was the symptom before it became a symptom?" Feel that world and live there.

TEN

Touch and Entanglement

I, you, he, she, we . . .
In the Garden of Mystic Lovers,
These are not true distinctions.[74]

Jelaluddin Rumi, the famous Islamic mystic, wrote these words during the thirteenth century. Rumi knew that your definition of yourself is entangled and created in part by interactions with everything and everyone.

From the nonconsensus reality viewpoint, that is, when you are lucid about the Dreaming, you experience yourself not only as a person, but also as a nonlocal entity, as relationships.

Every time you think about being a relationship and not a person, your everyday little self insists that this is only perennial philosophy, not real life. But then, Dreaming experience gives you different impressions. From the viewpoint of deep meditation experience, you know that your thoughts and your feelings, in fact your self and your energy, arise in

---

[74] From Coleman Barks and Michael Green's beautiful *The Illuminated Rumi* (New York: Broadway Books, Bantam, 1996), 60.

connection with everything around you, everything that catches your attention.

This chapter and the next explore the experience of being nonlocally entangled with another person or object. To begin with, we will explore experiencing yourself as part of another person's body with the use of subtle touch and investigate how sentient experiences merge individual processes.

RELATIONSHIP WORK REVIEW

To gain perspective on the meaning of sentient relationship work, it may be helpful to first gain an overview of other ways of processing relationship issues. For the sake of brevity, I will limit my overview to summarizing process-oriented methods of relationship work. The reader needing more information on any one aspect, such as transference, dreaming up, or signal work, may refer to the footnotes on those subjects.

1 and 2. Projection and Transference:
Projection refers to one-sidedly attributing your own feelings, ideas, and attitudes to other people or objects—especially externalizing blame, guilt, or responsibility. Projection is based on the assumption that who you are is separable from the other person.

Transference is the technical name for a projection within a therapeutic context. Freud's idea of the transference involves "transferring" feelings or desires related to your childhood and parents onto a teacher or authority figure in the present. Projection differs from just thinking about someone in that a projection is accompanied by a lot of emotion. You not only believe that something is true only for the other person or object, but are also disturbed, excited, or furious about it.

There are various methods of working on the transference. Some therapists use it as a central process by letting the troublesome projections or transference be. It is believed that the client needs to transfer feelings onto the therapist, who remains neutral, giving the client a chance to discover and express parental projections. For example, if you were my therapist and I experienced you as my mother or father, then you would just let me focus on the various feelings I had about you until they resolved themselves.

Other therapists do not work with the transference directly but enter into relationship processes, not as neutral beings or objects of projection, but as their real selves. Each therapist-client pair is different. Even in the same school of therapy, no one deals with transference the same way with each person.

3. Countertransference:

This occurs when the helper or teacher or therapist has strong feelings toward the student or client, especially around their transference issues. Since the healer's feelings toward the client partially determine how well the therapy goes, countertransference feelings are crucial to what occurs. If you have good feelings toward your client, that person is more likely to accept your medicine or therapy, whatever it is. When the countertransference turns negative or you cannot separate your experiences from theirs, the outcome is unpredictable and depends on awareness on all sides.

RANK:
The Boss and the Employee

4. Power and rank:

Every relationship involves differences of power and social rank, although we rarely focus on these unless there is trouble in relationship. One party always has more and the other less in areas of experience, education, economic opportunity, and so forth. Gender, race, religion, economic status, education, sexual orientation, age difference, and health issues give one person greater power over another at certain moments. Awareness of difference is crucial to using power, so that it forwards rather than disconnects people.[75]

The cartoon shows a woman (someone who generally has less social rank) putting down a white man (someone who has more social rank, at least in the West). One view of the cartoon is that she, as the boss, is misusing the rank she has as a boss. But from another viewpoint, the cartoon shows her seeking revenge for having been put down herself.

The delicate and intricate balance of rank in each relationship event is a complex and important background to communication that changes from moment to moment. As the cartoon shows, rank can be a serious issue, and its misuse is painful. For this reason, abuse is always a potential issue in relationships with rank differences. Regulations, laws, and civil rights are created to protect the one with less rank against those with greater social and economic rank. In therapy, these rights protect the client against the helping professional's misuse of rank.

However, rules and laws are not enough to protect us from projection, counterprojection, love, and rank misuse. At best, rules and laws in therapy serve to wake people up to the unconscious use of power. But without moment-to-moment awareness in individual situations, general rules have little value.

5. Dreaming Up:

Dreaming up is different than projection and countertransference. Dreaming up occurs when my dreams

---

[75] See my *Sitting in the Fire* for more on rank and power.

unwittingly provoke your feelings—without you or me realizing that your feelings are related to my dreams. In other words, your feelings are not created by your psychology alone, but are temporarily provoked or dreamed up by things that I do unconsciously and that you can see in my dreams.

For example, a client who dreams of a needy child may dream up a therapist to have positive feelings toward him or her. The therapist can locate the origin of these positive feelings by examining the dreams of the client. In this case, the client's "needy child" may be thought to "dream up" the therapist to have positive feelings.

Conversely, the client can also be dreamed up to behave in a certain way, because of the therapist's dreams. Take a therapist who does not like herself. You as a client may find yourself compensating for her lack of self-love by constantly feeling pressed to say supportive or loving things to her.[76] It is not always possible to disentangle exactly what is projection, countertransference, or dreaming up. These processes are "entangled" because of the Dreaming background.

Working with entanglement is a great challenge to awareness. I remember a startling example of entanglement from some years ago, when I was a training analyst in Zurich. One of my clients was a therapist herself. She came to see me because she felt unusually depressed. After she worked with me on her problems, she eventually told me about a case of her own. One of her male clients wanted to commit suicide, but had not been suicidal before he met her. She told me that she tried to help him, but her own depression made it difficult for her to do so.

As his therapist, she resisted discussing her own depression with him. However, one day, after her client told her that her moods were upsetting him, she mustered up all the courage she had and decided to speak about herself. In

---

[76] For more on dreaming up, see Joseph Goodbread's *Radical Intercourse* (Portland, Oreg.: Lao Tse Press, 1997).

an apparently dramatic interaction, she revealed her own depression to him. To her great surprise, he was delighted that she had these problems as well and decided to help her.

The two decided to switch roles! His therapist—my depressed client—became his client. Can you follow that? She became the client of her suicidal "client" and paid him for six sessions in which the roles were reversed.

He was infinitely more helpful to her than I had ever been! Moreover his helping her helped him. After those six sessions they switched back to their original roles, and she became the therapist again. His suicidal feelings disappeared, and later he too decided to become a therapist.

Not all entangled situations are as dramatic or end as well as this example. Nevertheless, there are always moments when relationships switch, when the one in need of help becomes the helper, the student educates the teacher, and so forth. Role switching plays a crucial part in every relationship, even though most people ignore the feelings that would make them switch.

By the time you become a teacher, you are in danger of getting attached to the power and social privilege involved. Because we all enjoy having authority and feeling powerful, we must be careful not to marginalize awareness of entanglement and role switching. Unconsciousness of attachment to power makes it easier, at least in some ways, to be a less privileged client, student or revolutionary than it is to be a teacher unconscious of her position. Awareness and detachment are needed by all.

Projection, dreaming up, transference, countertransference, and rank are terms that speak about people as if they were disentangled or at least only mildly entangled. However, in fact, some degree of entanglement is always present; you cannot always tell who is who. Working through the resulting confusion, entrapment, and role reversal requires a great deal of awareness and flexibility on the part of everyone concerned.

Because there is little support for such fluidity in relationships, there is little awareness of entanglement intricacies.

Nevertheless, when they are worked through with lucidity and consciousness, such situations can bring incredible learning and healing. In the case I mentioned earlier, both my client and her client improved. Without awareness, however, entanglement can lead to less-positive results.

I use the term entanglement in part because of its application in quantum physics. Entanglement in physics refers to the difficulty in differentiating quantum processes, that is, differentiating the state of one particle from the state of another particle. "Nonlocal" and "lack of independence" are other terms for entanglement. Nonlocality refers to two spatially separate processes that appear to be linked as if they were right next to one another.

In the case of human signals, entanglement results from the sentient state prevailing during the exchange of signals. Entanglement describes the difficulty in deciding who did what first. For example, did you smile as a reaction to my posture? Or was my posture a sentient reaction to something happening between us that preceded your smile? Since the origin of all signals is sentient, only their outer manifestations can be tagged first or second.

From one viewpoint, each of us is to blame for what happens between us; from another viewpoint, there is no blame, no single cause. Our relationship and its signal exchange is just a part of the Dreaming. By becoming lucid and conscious, we can best unfold that Dreaming in ways useful to all.

6. Signal Exchange:

In addition to the transference, countertransference, dreaming up, and the entanglement of all these processes, signal exchange itself is a specific way of working with relationships. In working on signal exchange, you first try to locate the origin of signals in time and space, knowing that their location and timing marginalizes the sentient background.

Signals work determines who did what. In particular, you watch for unintended or double signals. Unintended or double signals, such as smiling when you are angry, almost always results from the culture of the relationship, from the implicit lack of freedom or agreement that certain things cannot be shown or discussed. Signal work checks out the significance of the double signal, in this case, anger, and the reason why it seems impossible for the sender to clearly feel and express the double signal.[77]

7. Edge Work:

If you felt free, if there were no "edges," you would simply be angry when you were angry, rather than smiling. Edges are neither good nor bad; they are simply the reason signals are driven underground. Instead of working on signals, relationships can be enriched by asking about the sense of freedom in relationship. Lack of freedom creates edges or energy thresholds. These boundaries make it difficult to send certain signals or to identify with them.

For example, if you are afraid of me, you will not be able to express certain things and will have to keep them secret. But processes do not disappear; they simply become less apparent. "Secret" feelings emerge through unintended signals such as fear or anger. At this point, you can either work with the signals (and encourage them to come out) or work with the larger issue in the background, namely what is creating fear in the relationship. Focusing on this larger issue is edge work.

Signal work depends on seeing and hearing clearly, while edge work depends in great part on feeling clearly the sense of freedom or imprisonment at hand.

8. Big Dreams:

Except for the implicit entanglement in the background, the relationship work I have discussed thus far is based on separating and differentiating you and your friends.

---

[77] See my *The Dreambody in Relationships* (New York: Penguin, 1986) for more information about signal exchange.

However, when we speak of the dreams or myth behind relationship, it is impossible to separate the individuals.

The often life-long patterns driving relationships at any given moment can be intuited from memories of the first big experience or dream between two people. These memories and dreams show the overall structure of what is likely to happen later on.

The pattern seen in big dreams or memories is more decisive than I realized when I first discovered it.[78] The first experience that you have with someone, the time-we-were-just-getting-together, is mythic, especially when the other person says, "I remember that too." The first story is like a childhood dream, a root or seed for the relationship, and the rest of relationship is built around that seed.

I remember a professional couple with a large family who came to see me because they both felt a wall, or barrier, separating them. When I asked them about their first memory of the relationship, both remembered the first night they had slept together. They were at a party in a motel and tried to sneak away to a different motel room because they did not want their friends to know where they were.

However, when they wanted to come out of the room, the door accidentally locked and could not be opened from the inside. They could not get out! They were stuck together for hours, until the manager broke the door down to get them out. Moreover, in spite of their attempt to keep things secret, because of the excitement stirred up in the motel about their being locked in, everyone at the party discovered that they had slept together!

When I worked with them years later, both felt intractable barriers keeping them apart. When they told me the story above about being locked into that motel room, I decided to help them get back in touch with that myth, with the sense of being locked in. We all laughed until tears came

---

[78] I first discuss big dreams in relationships in *Dreambody in Relationships*.

to our eyes when they played the door that locked them in and I played the friends who discovered they were together. I believed that there must be something important in that locked-in experience and therefore suggested they go away together for two weeks to a remote island. I thought that locking them in again could be helpful. Moreover, they had to tell their kids and all their friends they were leaving town!

When the couple went away to the island, their problems disappeared. The barrier between them dissolved. The barrier appeared when they lost contact with the Dreaming that appeared in their "myth" and became normal, busy, professional people. The moral of this story is that getting in touch with our first dream or memory in relationship is helpful. These mythic patterns help us contact the deeper dreaming between us. Such dreams and memories belong neither to one person nor to the other, but to the "entanglement" in relationships.

The diagram on page 153 summarizes the various relationship methods. It includes method number 9, Sentient Entanglement, which I will discuss next. There are many more kinds of relationship work, including communication theory, structural family analysis, and field theory, all of which are quite useful in certain moments and situations. The foregoing methods are merely the briefest outline of some of the main process-oriented methods.

9. Sentient Entanglement:

You may have noticed that in the first seven methods, people and signals can be differentiated from one another, in spite of the entangled background to relationships. In the latter two methods, separation of individuals becomes impossible.

Now let us focus on sentient relationship work. Sentient work involves sensing the subtle atmosphere between people before it reveals itself as a signal from one person or the other. While the first seven methods are useful ways of solving problems, sentient work focuses on the unifying element of relationship; this method is a type of awareness training.

RELATIONSHIP METHODS

1. Projection—Integrate what has been put outside yourself.
2. Transference—Discover what the client projects on a helper.
3. Countertransference—Discover what you project on a client.
4. Rank—Discover Powers and how they are used.
5. Dreaming Up—Find your signals in the other's dreams.
6. Signal Exchange—Find unintended signals.
7. Edge Work—Explore where people feel imprisoned and free all.
8. First Dreams—Discover the myth of the couple.
9. **Entanglement—Sentient Work with Body and Visual Signals.**

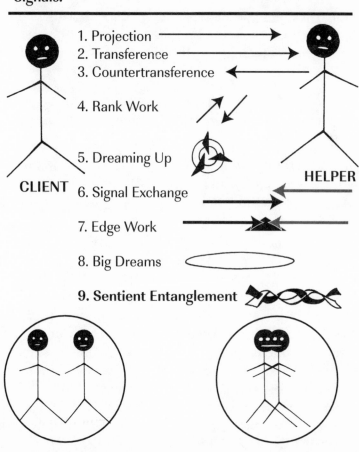

1. Projection
2. Transference
3. Countertransference

4. Rank Work

5. Dreaming Up

CLIENT 6. Signal Exchange

HELPER

7. Edge Work

8. Big Dreams

9. Sentient Entanglement

8. First Dreams   9. Sentient Entanglement

Sentient work explores the Dreaming connecting people, beneath the area of "problems." There are many ways of working sentiently. You can simply sense the atmosphere; you can work with addictive tendencies, or visual flirts, as we will explore in chapters 11 and 12. Or, you can use your touch, as we will now explore.

An easy way to begin sentient work is by retraining your touch to become lucid. I am going to invite you to use a special kind of touch to sense preverbal, prematerial experiences that are trying to happen or are happening between you and a friend.

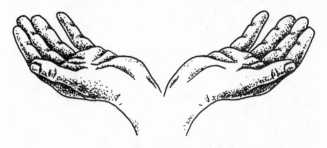

Sentient Touch Awakens Lucidity In the Hands

Sentient interaction takes place in a nonconsensual realm, where you easily move through, over, or under the other person's boundaries. Therefore, before working with someone in the way I will be describing, you should first obtain their permission.

Please remember that some people are body shy; they are not used to being seen or touched, much less focused on with subtle touch. Ask where you can touch them. In general, the back area is usually a good area to start.

For example, let us say you begin by putting your hand on someone's back. At some particular point while you are scanning or touching their back, let us pretend you suddenly feel something bony, something you cannot quite formulate. If you feel something bony, the next step will be to experiment with relating to the bony thing you are feeling by exploring its essence, its tendency, or root. Perhaps the essence of that bony thing feels to you like a tendency to point something out, to make a point, to be clear.

Your everyday mind will suggest to you that you are projecting something onto the other when you mindfully focus on the experiences you sense coming from their body. In sentient work, do not fight with your everyday mind. Just notice it. Remember your worries about projection, transference, countertransference, signals, edges, myths, or telepathy, but do not focus on them further just now.

With the other's prior permission, let go of your everyday mind and go into what you are experiencing. The sentient essence revealed by your touch is the point.

Once you are familiar with your sentient experience, attempt to describe it in words to the other person. Being vague is inevitable and even helpful. Say something like "I feel something bony, bonelike. Perhaps this is a piece of metal or a stick?" Take a guess about your sentient experience; formulate it in everyday terms. "Is there something wanting to point something out back there? Is it clarity, pointedness?"

As you sense and relate the sentient essence of your touch to the other person, her or his body will respond. You might feel new experiences coming from them; perhaps you will feel the temperature of their body change, or you may feel the muscles and tissue readjust under your sentient touch. Perhaps your friend will respond verbally as they discover and can relate to what you are talking about. Be lucid. If you feel and describe the sentient essence behind what you are experiencing, you will connect to the other person's Dreaming. It is an incredible experience that connects the two of you.

THE TWISTED ARM AND THE FISH

I remember working with a man I had never seen before. I gently rested my hand on this man's arm and immediately sensed something I can only express in terms of a twist. I thought at first that his muscles or tendons had been twisted and found myself fantasizing that his arm had been twisted. I told him that I experienced his arm as having been twisted, even tortured. To my surprise, he responded that his arm had been twisted out of its socket some years back. Was this twist his process or my own? Without asking him this question, he agreed to go further, and the two of us began dreaming together. We entered into a playful fight. We wrestled, gently twisting one another's arms, spoke, and playfully boxed until he completed a fight that began long ago. He related a painful story about having been beaten and hurt and unable to fight back. Now, as we reviewed that scene, he fought back and felt relieved.

His story reopened traumatic events from my own childhood. As I told him about the twisted-arm experiences I had had, he could go more deeply into his. As he did that, I found myself going more deeply into my own! Who was working on whom? Sentient touch had connected us to a process that was neither his nor mine, but both of ours.

I recall another example of a shy friend. At one point during our work together, with his permission, I put my hand on his back, on the top of his shoulders. To my surprise, I had the irrational feeling that I felt something soft, fishlike back there! As I began to describe this fishlike being, to my delight, the man instantly responded. He told me that astrologers told him he was a Pisces, a fish! See the picture below.

You may know that, according to astrologers, people born between February 19 and March 20 are considered to be Pisceans. The image of two fish swimming in opposite directions connected by a rope symbolizes the twelfth and final sign of the zodiac, Pisces. Astrologers believe that the tension created between these two fish swimming in opposite directions represents the tendency toward vacillation that characterizes the typical Piscean. Such people are kind but always shifting. Because of this inward duality, Pisceans frequently do two things at once and may lack the one-sided drive that other people use to reach goals.

Pisces

In this body work encounter, I honored that fish in him and discovered that he had trouble loving the fish part of himself. He was shy about his flexible, fishlike, fluid behavior.

But the fish was not only his process; it was mine as well. Though I am not a Pisces, I have Piscean qualities. I feel the inner fish above the water connected with the one below the water. When I am doing work in public, I may seem extroverted but feel very internal. People often think I am extroverted because they see me working in the world. Others think I am introverted because they see me disappear beneath the water to write for many weeks. But, in fact, I am not only internal or external. I have both sides, a fish below and above the water.

I related all this to my friend who totally understood me, just as I was able to comprehend who he is at the deepest level. Who was working on whom? My friend and I are different, but we are also the same. My friend is a Pisces; I am not a Pisces, but I also am! Knowing this connected us in an incredible way.

EXERCISE—LUCID TOUCH

Trying it yourself is the best way to understand lucid touch and entanglement. To awaken the lucid awareness in your hands, let us first experiment with using your hands on a piece of material or a piece of your own clothing. Take a moment and sensitize your hands to your own clothing. You probably do not spend much time feeling the things you wear or the materials around you, so take a moment now and choose something to touch.

Part I. Sensitizing Your Hands

Take the material in your hands and relax. Take a few minutes. Let your mind and your hands be clouded, unfocused.

Now, using your hands, explore the sentient essence inside the material you are touching. What is in there? Be lucid about the sentient nature of your touch and experience what flirts with your hand. Gently touch and notice your sentient experience. You need go no further just yet. Take your time.

This is not ordinary touch. Sentient touch is different, more irrational. You need to encourage yourself to experience things that may make no sense at first.

Once you experience the tendency inside the material, help that sentient experience unfold. Pretend that it is the seed of some creation trying to emerge and that your hands can sculpt and bring out this creation. Use your artistic ability; let your hands discover, then express what is in the material. Let your process unfold by itself. Help bring the experience into consciousness. Perhaps you can make up a story about a person who was looking for this, found it, and used it in life.

Look at what you have brought out of the material. In what way can this thing you created be a part of your life? How could you use it and live it more? Take time with this. Try to answer these questions. How can the object or form that came out of that material become a useful part of your life?

Now that your hands are sensitized, we are going to work similarly again, this time on the Dreaming shared with another person. You can begin by using your hands to sentiently touch the other, after asking where, when, and how you may touch. Notice what flirts with your attention. Remember that in working with another, your mind may say, "you can't do this." In a way, your mind is right. You can't—but your sentient awareness can. When you put your hands on the other, notice that while you are speaking of your sensations in an open manner, their body will give you feedback. Their body will speak to you. Wait for their conscious voice to say "yes." Then follow the flirting and beeping you feel in their body.

Do not forget that what you experience is neither you nor the other, but both. You are not working with the other, but with the combination of the two of you. Their story and experience will feed yours, just as yours will feed their process. Each story deepens and helps the other go over edges. Two stories are happening at once. This is an experiment in relationship—one body, one person, and two psychologies.

Part II. Working Sentiently with the Other

Sit or stand near your friend and begin by allowing yourself to enter into a clouded state. Then, using your sentient awareness, when your hands are ready, place them slowly and gently on the other person, on an area they have suggested. Detect tendencies, essences, and sensations from the other person's body. What sensations flirt with your attention? What do your hands feel attracted to or repelled by in the other?

Once you find the Dreaming flirt or tendency, with the other's permission, use your hands to sculpt and bring out the essence of the sensation that has flirted with you. For example, if you felt something like a plant, bring the plant out. If you felt something like a rock, create an imaginary stone with your hands.

Describe the sentient experience in words, the tendency behind what you have sensed, and check on the feedback from your friend. If you are clouded, sentient and lucid, the other will give you good feedback about connecting to something in them. This is a very irrational procedure; it can hardly be described in words. Your body and that of the other will lead you.

Dream together. Ask the other to be sentient and lucid as well and to join you in unfolding your combined experience in movement, storytelling, and art. Take time. For example, once I described the fish that I sensed in my friend's back, we described, fantasized, and even moved like fish until we had "sculpted" it and dreamed it together.

Help the other to process the experience as if it were only their process. Make space for it, talk to and about it, and relate to the experience that has unfolded. Ponder the meaning of recent dreams. Then relate your own experience, speak about yourself. Describe how the experience is also a part of your process.

Finally, explore the shared nature of the experience, dance, or story. In what way is the process that unfolded both yours and that of the other? Explore entanglement, the two processes as one, remembering that your relationship with the other person is a field that has always been there.

You and I belong to a more complete relationship process. Perhaps together we are a single being, the Dreaming. We may work on one of us, yet there is one spirit unfolding through two beings. When we work sentiently with our hands, the Dreaming background to relationship easy to understand and experience. But it is also easy to marginalize. Therefore, the next step in 24-Hour Lucid Dreaming is to notice how you are related to all things, knowing you are the material around you. You are not only your friends, you are also your bicycle, your car, the road, the motors, the plants, and all the animals.

 ## THINGS TO REMEMBER

"Entanglement" in quantum physics means you cannot differentiate the state of one particle from the state of another particle.

"Nonlocal" is another term for entanglement and lack of independence. Nonlocality refers to two spatially separate processes that appear to be linked as if they were right next to one another.

When you do sentient bodywork, your everyday mind will suggest that you are projecting something onto the other. Do not fight with your everyday mind. Just notice it. Remember your worries about projection, transference, countertransference, signals, edges, myths, or telepathy but do not focus on them while you do sentient bodywork.

ELEVEN

Addictions and Relationships

Why does he (the Commander of the Army) . . . have
only one foot?
Was it the work of heaven or of man?
The Commander said, "It was the work of heaven, not
man. Heaven made me one-footed.[79]

According to the commander with one foot, the Tao, rather than the enemy, cut off his foot. In the commander's mind, body problems do not come from oneself or others, but are entangled with the entire field. Perhaps the easiest way to see the connection between body feelings and the Tao, or atmosphere, is to look at addictions. In this chapter, we will explore the aspects of your addictive tendencies that are connected with the field you live in.

GENERAL CONSIDERATIONS

Speaking about addictions is treading on dangerous territory, because everyone has them. In general, we tend to

---

[79] *Chuang Tsu*, 57.

feel either that we are experts in this area or that we have no addictions. Addictions and addictive tendencies are a serious health problem, not only because they are so troublesome, but because some tendencies are so subtle that they are scarcely noticed.

First of all, let us agree on what we call an addiction. Let us say an addiction is a state of mind in which you take more and more of some food or substance to get the same desired effect, and that this state of mind endangers your health or relationships. In contrast to an addiction, an addictive tendency is a state of mind in which you are compelled to take more of a substance to get the same effect, but which does not immediately endanger your health or relationships. Relationships and health cannot be divided, because if your relationships are upset, your health will eventually be upset. The reverse works as well.

An addictive tendency is not immediately harmful but could possibly be. For example, many people eat too much salt. Salt may not immediately bother you, but it aggravates many problems. Eating less salt may relax you or lower your blood pressure. The picture below shows how eating less salt may reduce your blood pressure.

Salt is a Tendency toward Addiction

In the 1980s Amy and I discovered that everyone has two types of addictive tendencies. One tendency supports your identity, while the other supports your opposite. In other words, the foods and substances you are most attracted to support either your everyday identity or your secret, unacknowledged identity in dreamland.

For example, if you identify as a speedy person, you will tend towards foods and substances that stimulate you, such as coffee, because these support your primary identity. However, the more complicated, dangerous, and persistent addictions are linked to the "not-you" or secondary processes, to slowing down. One substance that may support slowing down is alcohol.

However, if you identify as a slow or depressed person, you might like substances or habits that keep you down, such as overeating. Your more serious addictions, however, will be linked to foods and substances that speed you up, such as sugar or caffeine.

The most difficult addictions are linked to unknown parts of yourself. Because these parts of you are marginalized, they can attract your attention only through seduction; they flirt with you and make you think about them because your conscious mind refuses to identify with marginalized states.

Many addictive food tendencies, like eating French fries or potato chips, do not have immediate negative consequences, but such tendencies may disturb your blood chemistry over time. Blood chemistry is a subtle disturbance; you do not notice or think about it until it clogs up your blood vessels after many years have passed. Without lucidity, you may not recognize how eating greasy foods can be an addictive tendency or an addiction.

At this point in history, Western medicine focuses on repairing your blood vessels and heart and usually ignores the subtle nature of addictive tendencies that create the biochemical basis for many physical symptoms.

METHODS OF WORKING ON ADDICTIONS

There are many ways of working with addictions. Each culture has its own methods, so you cannot recommend one method for everyone. Each person, culture, or subculture is different.[80] How to work on addictions and addictive tendencies depends on the individual, culture, age, and state of health. Any description of treatment for addictions, short of an entire encyclopedia, would be insufficient. Nevertheless, to describe sentient work on addictions, I must briefly, if inadequately, describe other major methods of addiction work.

Medical Interventions:

Someone with a long-standing addiction that is endangering their health must be encouraged to simply stop. There are various chemical supports and psychological treatments for stopping, ranging from just stopping oneself to the use of treatment centers for given addictions. Detoxification centers or "cleanup clinics," can be helpful in long-standing addictions where everything else has been tried. A clinic can provide medical help to detach from substances. At another point, once the immediate crisis has passed, it is crucial to work on the psychological and community origins of additions.

Community Work:

Addictions are connected to community problems. Wherever possible, working individually on addictions should be accompanied by working with the entire community. Like individuals, communities that live in a great deal of stress have severe relationship and addiction problems.

---

[80] Though many people have had excellent results from Alcoholics Anonymous, the San Francisco minister, Cecil Williams, who wrote *No Hiding Place: Empowerment, and Recovery for Our Communities* (San Francisco: Harper, 1994), talks about how Alcoholics Anonymous (AA) did not work in the African-American community. Because AA was based on white-European thinking and needs (such as "I am a powerless person"), instead of being based on African traditions and beliefs, Williams claims that AA was not effective with African-Americans.

Disenfranchisement, being put down and oppressed by more powerful groups, is a major factor behind addictions. Stressful management situations may also create addictions.

Organizations and communities with high performance expectations or high spiritual aspirations are typified by the holding of secrets. Where there are many secrets, addictions abound; in such situations, community work can be deeply healing.

Almost any group work involving the revelation of secrets, including revealing addictions and addictive tendencies, is helpful. Showing others your addictive tendencies is healing but difficult because addictions deal with deeply unconscious processes over which you do not have much control. Most people feel that lack of control is a sign of weakness and do not want to admit such a "weakness," even to themselves.

However, hiding addictions exacerbates them. Secrecy disturbs relationships, and disturbed relationships create stress and a greater tendency toward addictive tendencies.

Confrontation:

Chronic addictions are always accompanied by "self-denial." You think, "Who, me? I am not an addictive-type person." In other words, you may be constantly fooling yourself about your addiction problems and tendencies as well as about other health issues. You tend to think you do not have certain problems, even when you do. You have an "edge" to them, you suppress them. You say, "I've been eating, drinking or doing this for years, but let's face it, it's not that harmful. After all, I am still well, or at least alive." When you say such things, you are avoiding troublesome issues. If I feel my relationship with you can stand a confrontation, I will say; "You are fooling yourself! You're trying to tell yourself that this isn't harmful, but actually it's deadly. Don't lie to yourself. You are in the midst of committing suicide."

Strong relationships are needed to tolerate such confrontations. If two people feel connected, even devastating statements will be taken as an act of love.

Re-accessing Addictions:

Re-accessing is a method in which you think about an addiction and re-access the altered state of consciousness that it brings you. Take sugar. One way of re-accessing the state that sweet things bring to you is to sense the sweetness, exploring the feeling and atmosphere created by eating sweets. Re-accessing has proven to be quite helpful for people whose addictions are not severe. In the midst of severe situations, however, re-accessing may reactivate the need for the substance. There are many methods and combinations that are helpful with addictions. The list above is a broad and superficial overview of an enormous and complex field. See the summary below for methods of addiction work mentioned thus far.

ADDICTION METHOD	HOW TO DO IT
1. Community Work	Asking the Group to process tensions by representing polarities.
2. Confrontation	Confronting tendency towards self-denial and suicide.
3. Medical Intervention	Taking medication in or outside a clinical setting.
4. Stopping	Simply stopping, especially in a crisis situation and when all else has failed.
5. Re-accessing	Going back into experience of a substance.
6. Sentient Accessing	**Noticing addiction as a sentient tendency in relationship field.**

The directors of several clinics have told me that only 25 percent of people who work on their substance addictions in any kind of clinic are free from the addictions after ten years. There is definitely room for more research into the psychosocial-medical basis for addiction.

I want to focus now on a sixth method, "sentient accessing," that has been helpful even with long-standing addictions.

Let us explore the community field of relationships in which addictions take root.

SENTIENT ACCESSING OF RELATIONSHIP FIELDS

If you have worked on your addictions, it is likely that you have approached them as if they are "yours." Now, we will explore the connection between addictions and the world around you. This work will create awareness of what your body is craving in a given moment and explore the possibility that your body needs are connected to the atmosphere around you.

You will be giving addictions a lot of attention, a lot of room to express themselves, noticing their times and spaces. Remember, please, if you are telling yourself you have no addictions, you should really look again. We are all addicted to things, or have addictive tendencies. Go back to how you eat and how much or how little. Doing so could be crucial to your health. If you are eating too little, is this connected to the addictive tendency to eat too much? If you take medications for something, is this somehow related to addictive tendencies to certain foods that are bothering you?

Finally, note that the following meditation momentarily re-accesses addictive tendencies. If you are afraid of doing this exercise because it might exacerbate the addiction itself, increase your efforts at disciplining your awareness of tendencies and avoid acting on them directly.

SENTIENT ADDICTION WORK

Part I. Working on Yourself
Find a comfortable place to sit and choose one addiction or tendency to focus on. Remember that this can be something you are often compelled to take that upsets your health or your relationships or that tends to do so. It may be a substance or a food. Alternatively, choose the amount of

food you eat, if undereating or overeating is a tendency you have.

Now that you have chosen an addiction or addictive tendency, name it, that is, coffee, sugar, tobacco, alcohol, marijuana, and so forth. Next, recall the craving for that substance; feel that craving. What is the state of mind you hope the substance will create? Allow yourself to experience that substance, or rather the state you hope that substance will bring you now—without taking the substance. Can you feel that state in your body? Make some sort of movements that express that state.

Focus on the impulse behind the addiction, not on the addiction itself. The way to get to the tendency or impulse that exists before the addictive tendency arises is to remember the state you hoped that substance would bring. Again, make some hand motions that portray the state you hoped for. Now, slowly stop or let go of that motion, and just feel the energy or tendency left behind, the Dreaming that gives rise to that state.

This tendency, this Dreaming, is the sentient essence of your addictive tendency. Lucidly explore that Dreaming, the sentient impulse behind taking that substance. Explore the world at the sentient root of your addictive tendency. What does it feel like? What are space and time like at the sentient root of your addiction or addictive tendency? What is the atmosphere in that world? Live there, experience that right now. This is subtle work, give it time.

Now, ask yourself why you marginalize this experience so often and take a substitute, a substance, instead? In what way can you open up to this world and let it be present in your life? Make a note about this state and how to be more aware of its existence.

Work on the sentient essence, the Dreaming behind addictions, is the first part of our addiction work. The next step is to connect this work with relationships and community fields. The following exercise can be done in relationship, or you can imagine being with someone and going through the following experiences.

Part II. Community Field Work

Imagine the atmosphere around someone or some group where your addictive tendencies seem to emerge.

When you imagine being with the other person or group, imagine yourself working, talking, and being in that atmosphere. Notice exactly when your addictive tendencies arise. Ask yourself what you tend to be hungry for, what substance, food, drink, and smoke. What tendency arises within you?

Do not take this substance. Instead, *get to the sentient essence of the impulse behind the addiction.* Get into its essence, its preaddictive experience, its Dreaming.

How would the atmosphere in that relationship, group, or community have to change to reduce your addictive impulses? Imagine a new atmosphere in which your addictions would not arise. As you imagine and create this new atmosphere in your imagination, notice how the other person or people behave. How do they respond to the new atmosphere you are suggesting?

Finally, imagine inviting others to join you in creating a new atmosphere; dream together. Bring them into that new atmosphere. Let the other(s) join you in a drama, meditation, dance, story, or mad episode. Invite the others to follow their sentient experience as well.

Ask the others or imagine asking them, if and how their addictive tendencies are connected to the atmosphere the way it was and explore how the new change in the atmosphere affected them.

This experiment invites you to consider that everyone's body state is interconnected to the atmosphere in which you are living.

THE FORMAL PARTY

An example of two friends comes to mind; let us call them Rhonda and Sally. They worked with me on their addictive tendencies that came up at a formal party. The party went on too long and Rhonda ate too much, Sally drank too much. By the time they got home, they were both sick.

As we worked together, Rhonda explored overeating and found that the sentient experience in the background was hunger, excitement. According to her, people at the party were boring, too normal, too social and "conventional." Rhonda wanted something exciting to "bite into," so to speak. She marginalized her own excitement and ate instead. To change the atmosphere, she imagined inviting everyone at the party to talk about electrifying, creative things.

Sally had a different experience. As she focused on becoming lucid about the experience behind her addictive tendency to drink, she described the atmosphere at the party as "too formal"; it made her tense and drove her to alcohol. The essence of drinking was informality for her, freedom; to be as she wanted to be, say what she wanted to say. For her to get out of that formal atmosphere without drinking, everyone would have to forget their social rules and become unpredictable. She imagined everyone dancing wildly. To change the atmosphere, she imagined inviting people to drop their formal behavior.

The fascinating and common element behind both Rhonda's and Sally's experiences of the party was the uncomfortable social or formal atmosphere. Both women reacted with different addictive tendencies to compensate for that boring, tense atmosphere. Both people participated in, but really wanted to change, that atmosphere to get to the Dreaming behind the conflict between formality and individual experience. Instead of consciously recognizing this conflict and lucidly exploring the essence behind addictive tendencies, these two people, like most of us, simply marginalized the Dreaming.

The atmosphere affects us—each of us has states and processes that are linked to the entire environment. If you are lucid about your addictions and conscious of the conflicts in the atmosphere, you change yourself and can help the environment to change as well. Contact with Dreaming both reduces body problems, such as addictions, and addresses social issues. If you are lucid about your sentient experience, you know how to change the world. You know how you are that difficult world. You co-create the social atmosphere and its conflicts. In a way, your body can lead you to the solution, the Dreaming trying to emerge. In this way you are also a creative goddess or god who has us all in her hands, who creates people and the world. Furthermore, and perhaps most important, the separation between you and the divine is healed.

 THINGS TO REMEMBER

If you are telling yourself you have no addictions, look again. We all have addictive tendencies.

Explore the state you are addicted to. Do not take the substance, but lucidly experience the sentient impulse behind taking that substance and unfold it.

How must the atmosphere change in your relationship, group, or community to reduce your addictive impulses?

Your body is influenced by the Tao and can also take part in changing it.

TWELVE

Unbroken Wholeness in Relationships

If the Beloved is Everywhere,
The Lover is a veil.
But when living itself
Becomes the Friend,
Lovers, Disappear.[81]

According to meditation, Aboriginal thinking, quantum physics, and psychology, the background of what we call everyday reality is a complex nonconsensus reality (NCR) sentient interchange called the Void, the Dreaming, wave functions, or the unconscious. This sentient interchange between entangled parts is the root of reality, a root usually perceived only by poets and mystics. From their viewpoint, the NCR viewpoint, the everyday world is a huge, semihuman field of relationships, flirts, and flashes! Any one of us is then a "veil," as Rumi eloquently says. We are just the outer membranes of the sentient, nonlocal, universal essence beneath.

---

[81] *The Illuminated Rumi*, 127.

When the Dreaming unfolds, boundaries are created, there is a "you," an "I," and a "clock." But it seems that the world, that is, you and I, have consented to forgetting the Dreaming background of interconnectedness. When we forget this Dreaming, we are no longer the same as well as different, we are simply and completely separate!

Yet the sentient interchange between entangled parts makes it difficult if impossible to differentiate our processes from one another. In spite of our boundaries and rules, useful as they are, we are still confounded, amazed, awestruck, and furious with our entanglement. You could say that we have an entanglement issue.

Quantum physics has an entanglement issue as well. Entanglement appears most clearly in physics in the Bell's "one-world" theory.[82] Bell's formulation of nonlocality, and David Bohm's reformulation of it in terms of the unbroken wholeness of the field in which we live, can be seen in the famous experiment showing that individual particles of matter that arise at the same moment are eternally linked.

Particle A   Light Bulb   Particle B

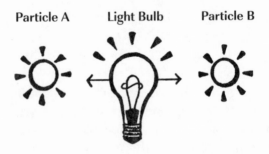

Consider the diagram above. There you see a light bulb and two particles of light, or photons, shooting out from either side of it. It turns out that if the two photons, particle A and particle B, are both created at the same time, they remain linked forever, wherever they may go. This nonlocality was

---

[82] Mentioned in chapter 5 in connection with "Not-Working on Yourself."

suggested by Bell's theorem and disturbed many; it would have disturbed Albert Einstein, were he still alive in the 1970s, because he argued against a universe in which nonlocality existed. Nevertheless, in the 1970s, Bell's theorem was tested and shown to be true in experiments performed by Alan Aspect. Though the experiments shocked many physicists, the results are generally accepted today, even though they remain unexplained.

Nobel Prize winner David Bohm reformulated the experiment in terms of a new hypothesis. He said that a background of "unbroken wholeness" links all parts of the universe. Other theorists considered possible explanations for the experiment, including particles that are superluminal, that is, move faster than the speed of light.[83] Regardless of how you explain it, the experiment and theory imply that since we are material objects and since according to the Big Bang theory, all matter was created more or less at the same time at the beginning of the universe, we are all inextricably linked.

While the debate about the nature of reality continues in physics, meditators and Aboriginal dreamers have always experienced our everyday reality of stones, trees, chairs, tables, and people as inherently connected. In other words, while we are different, we also experience an underlying interconnectedness. This chapter explores that interconnection in relationships using visual flirts, that is flickering, evanescent perceptions that last for only split seconds at a time.

VISUAL FLIRTS IN PSYCHOLOGY

Extrapolated to the human realm, one of the results of Bell's theorem is that we are all interconnected. Since all matter was theoretically created at the beginning of the universe, your photons, my photons, and the photons of all other objects in this universe are inextricably linked. We are

---

[83] See my *Quantum Mind*, chapter 18, for a discussion of the arguments around Bell's theorem.

interconnected with everything—the ground we walk on, the clouds above, the city we fly over, the pond we drive by, the ants we step on and the viruses we share.

Psychology has many kinds of nonlocality and its own analogies to Bell's theorem. Family theorists have long used field theories to predict how members of families and small groups are inextricably interconnected. Think of how the "identified patient," often projected onto the child in a family, plays the role of the suffering individual, which no one else wants to identify with. As soon as one of the adults picks up the suffering and speaks of herself or himself, the child frequently improves. All the parts of the system are interconnected.

Although as far as we know, Jung never considered field theory, he did have a sort of intrapsychic field theory. Jung noticed how the figures in the dreams of two people in a partnership are interconnected. In the days when hetero-sexuality was imagined to be the only normal, standard kind of relationship, partners—a woman and a man—were linked in dreams by a pair of lovers. Somewhat like the above pair of photons, Jung imagined the man's "anima" and the woman's "animus" to be inextricably linked. The anima corresponded to his inner dream female, and the animus to her male dream counterpart.

I would like to generalize Jung's theory to include all kinds of partnerships. Let us call any figure you feel attract-ed to in a dream an "inner companion." This inner compan-ion may be your present partner, a friend from the past, a potential friend of the future, or simply a fantasy figure with-out reference to everyday reality.

Jung realized that his animus and anima were linked like the photons described above; the behavior of the animus influenced the anima and vice versa.[84] Instead of

---

[84] In an oversimplified example of Jung's theory, if the woman's ani-mus (her ideas) was opinionated, the anima, (his feelings) became moody. If the anima was happy, the animus might be more related, and so forth.

speaking of photons, Jung spoke of dream figures. We can now say in a more inclusive manner that our "inner companions" are like virtual particles; they communicate with one another in an inexplicable manner. Letting go of the heterosexual bias allows us to say more simply that your feelings and ideas are connected to your partner's feelings and ideas. This is a particle theory in psychology, a dream-part theory.

While you and your partner are real people, the inner companions are virtual or dream parts whose effects can be seen in terms of the feelings, ideas, and gestures you make.

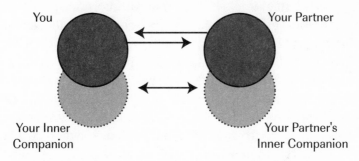

Unconscious Parts of Us Are Like Entangled Photons

While you and your partner communicate with one another by speaking, gesturing, and exchanging signals, which you can see on a videotape of your conversations, the inner companions manifest dreamlike aspects that flirt with one another.

Even if you and I as individuals do not flirt with one another in the social sense, dreamlike figures within us flirt. That is, parts of us that you can see in dreams exchange glances while we talk to one another. Flickering smiles, glances, quick sensations of embarrassment, hesitation, shyness, and boldness are flirts in the sense of almost invisible, evanescent experiences. We marginalize most of these flirts; we try to avoid staring at someone's body or clothing, yet we dress ourselves so that our clothes can catch someone's attention. Something about us wants to catch the attention of others and be known.

You may think that you organize what you wear. If you were more lucid about your sentient experience, however, you would probably notice that the material you choose to wear gives you sentient experiences that something in you feels connected to. Furthermore, the colors and shapes of your clothing portray what your conscious mind interprets as sexy, handsome, pretty, strong, spiritual, tired, sick, and so forth. Appearances are organized to flirt with one another, though the essence of these flirts can only be experienced with lucidity. Do not trust your conscious mind to interpret someone else's appearance, since you are likely to be wrong!

The diagram at left implies that flirting is an unconscious communication that you can experience in Dreaming at times in everyday reality and can also see in the figures of dreamland from the night. Thus we relate at various levels. We send intended signals, such as hello and goodbye. We send unintended signals, like gesturing sadness with a hanging head while saying we feel well. And we flirt with one another, with flickering sensations that precede visible communication or signals that happen so quickly that you cannot notice them on a video reproduction of a conversation. These flickerings come from the Dreaming, from the entangled state of unbroken wholeness.

We cannot break Dreaming or nonconsensual communication into parts and determine which dream figure or sentient experience belongs exactly to whom, or which person does what first or second. Thus we must conclude that we are entangled

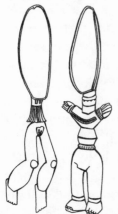

like twin photons. I call this indivisibility at the quantum level of relationships, "homosentience," that is, reflecting sameness. You and your partner may be very different at the everyday level, and yet you may manifest the same or similar characteristics in Dreaming.

From the lucid viewpoint in relationships, from the viewpoint of Dreaming, when I look at the thing about you that is catching my attention, I am looking at myself. In other words, from the viewpoint of the little me, I am attracted by myself in you. Or I myself attract me. Or you are me (or I am you). Only in everyday reality do we think we are attracted by our opposites. The diagram opposite, which comes from native people of the South Pacific, shows this essential sameness.[85]

From the viewpoint of my everyday focus on consensus reality, we are different. From the viewpoint of dreaming, what attracts me about you is what the little me forgot—it is the larger Self we share.

PISCEAN HOMOSENTIENCE

You may recall the example from chapter 10 in which I sensed a huge fish when I placed my hands sentiently on my friend's back. We then unfolded "Pisces-Dreaming" together. He told me about his Piscean nature, which stimulated me to speak about mine. We shared qualities that astrologers consider Pisceans to be: sensitive, emotional, sunny, impressionable, dreamy, creative, psychic, and mystical.[86]

A fish in my friend's back flirted with my sentient perception. That fish was invisible; you could not see it on a videotape of my friend. That fish was neither his nor mine, but an aspect of the Dreaming connecting us. In the empirical world of everyday reality, you cannot say who was the Pisces. But that did not matter to us; we were so happy just to be in the water!

Everything that flirts with you, whether it comes from a tree, a rock, or a person, everything that precedes

---

[85] From *Art Mania 10,000* (where no reference to a specific native people is made, probably because this picture is a sketch of native art).

[86] Under "Pisces (astrology)," (Microsoft® *Encarta® 97 Encyclopedia.* © 1993-96 Microsoft Corporation), you will read, "Pisceans tend to be idealistic; sometimes the real world gets too harsh and ugly for them. To escape unpleasant realities, some Pisceans retreat into their own dreams and fantasies and become evasive, even deceitful. Others escape productively through charity work, the arts, religion, meditation, and solitude. Pisceans make good listeners, can see different sides of issues, and often have great sympathy for the suffering of others."

observations, projections, and everyday reactions was first the Dreaming, which then unfolded.

THE LEVELS OF AWARENESS

Working with the sentient background to relationships and groups is "preventive" relationship medicine. If you catch the roots of experience, you reduce the dramatic nature of projections. Conversely, if you are not lucid about things that catch your attention from someone else, at another point, you will believe that those things (like the fish) are attached only to them—and not yourself!

Marginalizing your experiences is the beginning of projection. Most explosive and difficult situations in relationships could have been ameliorated if you remembered the unbroken wholeness that connects us.

The following exercise encourages you to be lucid in relationships. In what follows, you will be asked to verbalize the most subtle, flirtlike processes. Sitting, or imagining sitting, with someone else, you will begin by being clouded and then focus your attention on the atmosphere in the relationship. This may be new because you may not be accustomed to being clouded or to speaking about things that are difficult to verbalize. You will be using your awareness on subliminal, sentient relationship phenomena, noticing flickering aspects of the other person that catch your attention.

In past times and in Aboriginal cultures, shamans went into trances, played drums, and explored sentient, altered states of consciousness. They had cultural support, and their work was considered a crucial part of life. Today, you may find yourself working alone when you work sentiently on relationships. It takes courage.

In the training that follows, it may help to think that even though you should not talk about subliminal and irrational phenomena, when you express sentient experience, you are not really talking about yourself or anyone else, but about the field between you.

RELATIONSHIP AWARENESS EXERCISE

Begin as you usually do, hanging out or chatting with someone. Since you are reading this book in the moment, begin by imagining yourself chatting with someone you are interested in for one reason or another.

Be clouded and begin to meditate and report out loud on what the atmosphere between you feels like. Is it fun, heavy, depressing, scary, or something else?

Now, when you are ready, experiment with allowing the Dreaming atmosphere to appear in terms of flirts and flashes. You might need to relax and be clouded first. Close your eyes for a moment. Then, when you are ready, half open your eyes and gaze at the other person. Let your unconscious mind notice those flitting flashes that seem to come from the other person or from the area around them. Notice what flirts with you. Do not marginalize what you see or sense. Rather, become lucid about sentient experience.

Now focus on that flirt. Find its essence, the feeling atmosphere it generates. Do not stay with the outer thing, but get to its seed, its tendency. What you are focusing on is the mysterious field between you.

Now shapeshift. Try to sense and move into the world of the essence of the thing that flirted with you, that characteristic "of the other person." When you are ready, imagine that the flirting experience had a mind of its own. Become that characteristic of the "other" person; slip into its mind.

Finally, see yourself through its eyes. Give yourself a message, or let a debate occur between your ordinary self and the flirting essence. This may be very irrational, but allow 24-Hour Lucid Dreaming to occur. Look through its eyes, the eyes of that element of the "other" person that flirted with you, and give yourself a message. What is that message?

If you are able to enter into altered states of consciousness with the other person, and if they are willing, try dreaming together; unfold the common Dreaming together.

Afterward, consider how and why you both marginalize that experience. Discuss the atmosphere, the field between you, and the reason you both tend to marginalize that experience.

Be lucid of the atmosphere, and of the field you are living in. That atmosphere is Dreaming. Look at the other person; see how that atmosphere can appear in a flirt apparently coming from them. Appreciate that flirt as a part of yourself as well.

LOVE FOR YOURSELF

As I said earlier, working in a sentient manner on relationships calls into the question the common assumption that you are attracted to your opposite. As the above exercise shows, you are always in the process of being attracted to yourself. The objects and people that attract and disgust you are you. The method of 24-Hour Lucid Dreaming gives you the sense that everything you look at is your extended Self or community.

Normally, you identify yourself with your name. Your everyday mind probably thinks that the people who interest you are not you. Sticking to your everyday identity marginalizes the Big You and creates inner tension and outer conflict and misunderstanding.

In consensus reality we are separate. I am an individual. I am Arny and you are whoever you are. I come from this culture; I have this color skin, this gender, this sexual orientation, age, background, and so forth. We are different. There is an incredible beauty in our diversity. But this diversity is generated in part through marginalization of our sentient experiences. It is important to realize and stand for our differences. Yet, becoming conscious only of our consensus reality (CR) viewpoints and their political and social reality can marginalize the Dreaming. CR and NCR are two levels of reality that have been in an eternal struggle. History is the story of the struggle between difference and sameness, diversity and oneness. Most of us are not aware enough of diversity in CR or sufficiently lucid of our common Dreaming.

In my experiences with large group processes and businesses, processing the atmosphere in families, groups, and cities, I have seen how conflict has the positive effect of raising consciousness of difference. Awareness of social ranking systems can be a matter of life and death for those with lower rank.

Gaining consciousness of diversity is difficult enough. But you must not stop there. It is too little. You need to go further to the next step in relationship that involves discovering your differentness and *simultaneously discovering your sameness*. The more conscious you are of the other, the more you can appreciate their differentness. The more lucid you are, the closer you feel to everyone. You share the same fate as everyone who catches your attention.

Working with various native groups around the world has been an honor and a source of great learning for me. I have learned that members of these communities often treat one another on one level as if they are identical, as "family." When they say to one another, "sister and brother," they mean, in part, you are different than I am, but also the same. We are in the same family together with all sentient beings, which includes everything that catches our attention, with the pots and pans, the trees, cars, and animals.

Many of my readers come from cultures or family systems whose traditions still welcome simultaneous awareness of diversity and sameness, consciousness and lucidity. In these cultures, the plants and trees, animals and earth, are your relatives. There is a lot to learn from our Aboriginal relatives. Native traditions support experiencing the world sentiently and realize that whatever happens to anything or anyone is happening to you.

Be courageous in everyday contact and conversation; switch to Dreaming. Change the level of your communication; get to the sentient essence of your conversation. Speak about the atmosphere and the flirts. Take relationship as an opportunity. Take real people as the bright side of the moon, and the sense of being attracted or repelled by someone as the dark side of that same moon, as a chance to use 24-Hour

Lucid Dreaming to explore the sentient reality. Remember that our separate selves, the little you and the little me, your identity and mine, will surely die. But our sentient commonness is eternal; our relationship is nonlocal, timeless, and immortal.

Without lucidity, relationship problems will never be completely resolvable, and life and death will always remain the great dividers. With lucidity, however, there is no separation or death. You or your friend can never be parted because you are both always just arriving. This reminds me of a lovely phrase in a poem by Thich Naht Hanh, the Vietnamese Buddhist monk: "Don't say that I will depart tomorrow, even today, I am still arriving."[87]

 ## THINGS TO REMEMBER

We connect with one another sentiently like twin photons—we are entangled, interconnected, nonlocal, and everywhere.

It takes courage to follow flirts in relationship.

It takes even more courage to get to the essence of these flirts and not be hypnotized by their pictures on the bodies of everyday life.

The deepest relationship issues may be resolvable only with lucidity.

---

[87] From his beautiful text, *Please Call Me by My True Names* (Berkeley, Calif.: Parallax Press, 1993).

THIRTEEN

Dreaming As World Work

You must be the change you wish to see in the world.
—Mahatma Ghandi

By this point, you may have felt that 24-Hour Lucid Dreaming helps you create a greater sense of diversity and inner connectedness with all beings inside yourself, at least every now and then. But can it help you solve conflict in groups and in the world at large? Will the harmoniousness that comes from discovering you are the other not squash your consciousness of diversity and interest in social change?

While increased lucidity might at first glance seem to lessen our interest in social change, its effect is, in fact, the opposite. In this chapter, we will see how lucidity is needed to process diversity issues. In fact, without lucidity, the world will not change.

The problem is that the detached and mystic experience of lucidity, the feeling that you are the other, can, without consciousness, make you oblivious to conflict. That is why Marx called religion the opiate of the people. By focusing on eternity, you can easily skip the problems of today. Many mystics tend to look down on discord and opposition, implying something is wrong with the people involved.

In my experience, however, surviving and resolving severe conflict occurs most rapidly if you are simultaneously lucid about the Dreaming and conscious of the diversity that arises in connection with it. Enlightenment is indeed lucidity and consciousness and carries with it an amazement and delight in diversity. Alone, I am not enlightened, but together with you, we have a chance.

PUTTING MYSTICISM TO WORK IN SOCIAL ACTION

In our exploration thus far, we have grounded the mystical belief that you are the world in terms of empirical experience as well as in Aboriginal and Western science. Mystics from all religions, Taoists, Buddhists, and Hindus, as well as some quantum physicists, all agree that we are made out of one and the same matter, stardust. We all share the same parts in dreamtime; we are quantum entangled, difficult to separate in NCR. To bring these insights into everyday life, we need to practice living lucidly, noticing and getting to the essence of flirts to bring out the Dreaming and increase our acceptance of diversity.

HOT SPOTS

As an individual, you notice things flirting with your attention all the time. Without 24-Hour Lucid Dreaming, you tend to marginalize them. In this arena, groups behave just as individuals do. Let us call the moments that flirt with groups "hot spots." These are emotional moments that catch a group's attention but are too amazing or uncomfortable to focus on; hence, they are brushed over. To notice them, a whole group has to be lucid.

Imagine the following group process around racism. Social activists in a large, tense, open forum in the United States were arguing with a woman from a mainstream group about her ignorance of the history of oppression in her area. She stubbornly held her position and strongly resisted any responsibility for the sad history of oppressing disenfranchised people.

In her view, the social activists should be less angry and less vocal. Of course, this only inflamed nonmainstream group participants and activists who were trying to explain their situation to her. The scene escalated and stalemated.

In the midst of this heated situation, the bells of a nearby church began to chime. Everyone was quiet for a moment, heard the bells begin to chime, and then went on with the heated debate. The facilitators, however, were lucid. They caught those "flirting chimes" and asked the group to wait a moment while the bells rang. The facilitators asked the group to sense the ringing bells. Someone's voice suddenly broke the momentary silence and sounds of the chimes by quietly announcing that the bells reminded her of Christ.

The facilitators picked that up and "unfolded" the experience of the bells, suggesting that the figure of Christ might somehow be in the background atmosphere. They recognized that not everyone in the group was Christian, yet everyone spoke of Christ as a missing role, a necessary part of the overall diversity situation. They suggested that the sense of Jesus was present and asked if someone could speak for Him as if He were there. Others agreed and pretended for a moment that they were Jesus Christ, showing compassion for all human beings, for those who were oppressed in that city, and also for the oppressors, including the stubborn mainstream woman. The Jesus figures radiated such kindness that everyone had to listen.

The mainstream woman was touched; she broke down and wept. Everyone was silent. After a few minutes, she gave up her untenable position and asked everyone's forgiveness for what she had said. She admitted her responsibility in continuing the oppression and promised that she would make herself more aware of current social issues and interact with her own racist family.

When we are in groups, as well as when we are alone, the Dreaming flirts with us, trying to bring the background of unbroken wholeness into a world that is split into parts.

Being lucid about the sentient essence of flirting events and hot spots, such as the chiming bells, creates awareness and diversity tolerance. In this way, conflict and harmony, consciousness of parts and lucidity of the unitary background, are basic to finding resolutions to world problems.

Individual and Global Tao

INNERWORK AND WORLD WORK

Our world is like a pot of water on a stove, which frequently boils over because of tensions between polarized groups. These tense moments are a perfect opportunity for world work to begin. World work is a group work method based on the assumption of "deep democracy," namely that each voice and every feeling needs representation in order for a group to know itself and resolve its issues. The method of 24-Hour Lucid Dreaming is an additional way of realizing the potential of world work.

There are many moments to use your lucid awareness in the midst of family, group, or city processes. Watching for hot spots is one. Noticing the moments that flirt with the group's attention and getting to their sentient essence can lead to resolution, as the previous example demonstrates.

Asking the speakers in a group process to speak sentiently, from their deepest being, is another application of lucidity. Many people are too shy to speak in groups, and then, when they do, speak only from the viewpoint of their "little you" instead of lucidly from the viewpoint of the heart.

A third application is using awareness to notice when you are feeling like the "opponent." Once you have spoken, maintaining awareness in a group process means noticing whether you are still on your side, or whether you are unconsciously taking the side of someone else. If that is the case, then do it. Switch roles; you can even take your opponent's side.

For example, I remember a moving situation in a large group process dealing with racial issues. A conflict broke out between a younger gay white man who criticized an older African-American man for being too strong. The older man defended himself, and then, noticing how he really liked the courage the younger man had in speaking up, admitted that he liked the younger man and supported him in speaking out. The African-American man told the white man that he was growing into being an elder himself. The older man had apparently seen a flirt coming from the younger man. He noticed the younger man's power and joined him there. Instead of arguing, the older man stepped into that power, supporting the younger man and himself as well. It was an awesome moment to see two men, both from marginalized groups, begin by arguing and then end up admiring each other. That incident brought a whole group together.

Every time you notice something about the "other" that attracts or disturbs you, every time you explore that flirt and share it, you model Dreaming together, and role switching. In a way, you drop your own self-definition and extend it to include the common ground between yourself and the other person.

Dropping and extending your self-definition is a kind of shapeshifting. Shapeshifting is easier to talk about than to do because, when you get into tense situations, everyone becomes fascinated with consciousness and the overtly polarized diversity situation. To do world work you need a lot of inner discipline, practice, and meditation. One without the other is unsustainable.

The following innerwork practice will be helpful in moving through group problems with your family, group, and organization. It will give you the chance to notice various moments in group process where lucidity can be a great help.

Dreaming in World Work

Think of a family, group, organization, or business that is on your mind these days. Which of these communities catches your attention just now?

What is the atmosphere like in that group, or that part of the group? Is it rough, pleasant, tense, competitive, peaceful, or partylike?

Take a moment and ask yourself about the sentient essence behind that atmosphere. What lies behind the atmosphere, what is its root? What is the seed from which this atmosphere has grown? Is this "seed" represented in the group? How might you represent that seed and encourage others to do so as well? Write down a note about this seed.

Now let us focus on the outer roles in the field. Who or what is the ostensible issue? Who are the leaders, the followers, and the spiritual elders? Who feels put down, who are the oppressors? What other roles exist in that group? Who is in the marginalized role in your group?

Are you in conflict with any one person or role in that group? Take a moment and remember the behavior of the person or people in that role. What exactly upsets you about that person?

See them, and then experiment with trying to feel the way they feel. This is not easy, so be patient with yourself. What is the sentient essence of their feeling? Is this a part of yourself that you have marginalized? Feel your way into that role or person until you no longer marginalize this experience.

When you are ready, shapeshift; give yourself a chance to experience their role. How have you been playing this role unconsciously? This is a difficult question. Take a moment and think about it. Just notice, do not criticize yourself. Try shapeshifting into the role of the person you are in conflict with. Experiment with being them, behaving like them. Feel what it is like to be them, and try to understand where they are coming from.

Now let us focus on the group's possible hot spots. What events catch or could catch the group's attention every now and then? What are the hot spots it tends to gloss over? Identify one such hot spot and imagine focusing on it now with the whole group. Go into this event that flirts with the group. Unfold it in your own mind, imagine it going further, dream it on. How does the sentient essence of the hot spot compare to the sentient essence of the person or role that was bothering you?

Imagine maintaining your lucidity in a future meeting; imagine bringing one of your experiences of the sentient essence of a situation to the group process. Imagine speaking about the atmosphere, the sentient essence of person who was problematic for you; imagine being lucid about hot spots. (Remember the chiming bells as a hot spot in the beginning of this chapter.)

Remember your individual work in earlier chapters. Recall how working on events that flirted with you answered prayers you had not even formulated. Consider how unfolding that hot spot on the previous page may be a possible answer to the group's deepest and perhaps unformulated prayers. Imagine sharing this insight with the group the next time it meets.

Community tensions are a great challenge and an opportunity to enter into a journey of self-discovery together. What else can lead you and your world to become conscious of its parts and people, and towards 24-Hour Lucid Dreaming?

CONFLICT WORK WITH LARGE GROUPS

My psychology teachers thought it was crazy to deal with groups; better to leave them alone. It was thought that groups lowered one's mental level. My teachers were right, but they were also wrong. Groups do challenge your mental level, put you into altered states of consciousness, make you feel things you did not want to, remind you of your fear, hatred, anger, ambition, pride, humiliation or greed. Groups can be terrifying. That is why many people avoid large group processes.

But these altered states are not just problems but solutions as well. My suggestion is not to marginalize these problems because they are uncomfortable. Become lucid and conscious, embrace the problem, go down into it, get deeper, and explore the states and people who flirt with you, get to the sentient essence, and help everything transform.

All this may sound easier to learn than it is. When I first started to work on diversity issues, most of what happened was pure conflict. To make things worse, my colleagues from other psychological communities criticized me. Some thought I was ruining psychology, or at least ruining process work. Why open up to all those social problems? But I had no choice. What were my options? I could either open to all those problems, learn how to be of service, and change myself, or get hopeless and criticize the world for being unconscious and violent.

In this spirit of lucidity and consciousness, I suggest group work to everyone interested in social action and psychology, world change and meditation.[88]

You need inner work to track the feelings you have in group work. It is important to notice and remember how you feel pulled into one role or another in a field, because they are all potential forces within you. Being lucid about your sentient experience allows you to comprehend diversity and

---

[88] Details of world work can be found in my *Year I: Global Process Work with Planetary Tensions* (New York: Penguin-Arkana, 1990), *The Leader as Martial Artist: An Introduction to Deep Democracy, Techniques and Strategies for Resolving Conflict and Creating Community* (San Francisco: HarperCollins, 1992), and *Sitting in the Fire*.

Briefly, the elements of world work include atmosphere, roles, rank, and crazy wisdom. As I have said earlier, it is important to notice the overall feeling atmosphere in a room. This atmosphere may be tense or relaxed. Lucidity about the sentient atmosphere watches how this atmosphere unfolds into polarities, such as the oppressor and the oppressed, the teacher and the student, the boss and the workers, and so forth.

Discover how the field manifests in terms of roles and how important rank and awareness of those roles are. Unconsciousness of the role you play and the rank it has in your social setting creates tension and fear.

You also need to use your lucidity to notice fun, crazy wisdom, and celebration. (In some places, the field is really intense and feels very serious and thick and it may seem forbidden to lucidly perceive the whole

switch roles consciously. All of us are really too big and have too many sides to be stuck in one role. Only your everyday identity inhibits you from role switching by insisting that you are you and your enemy is out there.

Remember Feynman's diagrams for particles in a magnetic field? An electron enters a field and suddenly other roles are created. A fluid electron, a lucid one, feels the field, switches roles by picking up the nature of its antimatter opposite, the positron, and steps out of time. This means in effect, that it steps out of its normal CR role. Quantum physics suggests that you can do the same—you can try being sentient and switching roles!

---

scene as if it is a divine unfolding. You may need to apologize to consensus reality and explain your detachment before sharing your view that the world is a divine puppet theater, and most of us are its puppets.)

When there are many issues that are competing with one another, filter through them, asking people to vote on the one they wish to address first. Since we work sentiently, that is by noticing the feeling, it turns out that almost all the roles and issues are entangled. You cannot solve financial issues without addressing social rank; you cannot address rank without addressing sexism and racism, you cannot work on these issues without focusing on economics and homophobia.

Once you identify an atmosphere or an issue, different roles, or polarities, appear, that is, the different viewpoints within those issues will arise.

For example, if you have an environmental problem in a city, there are some people who are on the green side of the issue and want to preserve the environment, and on the other side is business or logging or development. These different polarities create a particular atmosphere or feeling in the moment.

There are always ghost roles. For example, if your group gets together and starts to discuss an environmental issue and some people speak about the children or the trees who might be affected by that environmental problem, then the children and the trees are ghosts, if they are not directly able to speak. They are roles that are spoken about but nobody is embodying them yet. Roles in a field are virtual; they are felt, but you cannot have complete representation in a deep democracy without representing everyone and everything. So all ghost roles must be filled in a deep democracy. In this case, this means that people must step into the roles of the kids and the trees and speak!

GROUP WORK IN IRELAND

Role switching has immense power; it avoids annihilation, not just among elementary particles, but in group processes as well. A startling scene from our conflict work in Ireland shows how powerful role switching can be.

We had originally planned to work in Belfast, but the suburb that hired us experienced too much violence to organize the conflict resolution meeting. A couple months before we were to work in Ireland, the process work group from Dublin took over and organized a seminar in Dublin. Approximately two hundred people from all over Ireland met in a large theater in Dublin just two days before the 1998 peace accord was signed. I remember one unusually intense scene from the group processes occurring during those days.

After several speakers had discussed the issues from the northern and southern perspectives, a man from Ireland became embroiled in a heated conflict with a political activist from Northern Ireland. Both were fighting each other with words, screaming while everyone else huddled around them.

Each spoke of the wrenching pain of having had to witness their family killed by the opposing party. Each had suffered injury from bombs. Neither man wanted to stop raging. One even said that he did not plan to ever stop. This was the first time he had spoken to a man from the other side for twenty-five years.

At one point, the man from the north insisted that even though he was from Britain, he was still an indigenous Irishman. This statement was like a bomb, and all hell broke loose. The man from the south, red in the face, screamed at him in an unending, entangled tirade. Meanwhile, the group cheered, supported, or jeered the men as they went on. It was if the unspoken were finally emerging.

But then I remembered consciousness and lucidity. The bright red color of the neck of one of the men flirted with me. Then I noticed how red the other man was as well. I caught that apparently irrational flirt and asked myself why they were both so red. Inside myself I reflected and knew why I was so red; I was terrified, furious, afraid of violence and death. I felt death haunting me.

I asked one of the men about that redness in his neck and to my shock and the amazement of all present, the man whom I had addressed stopped yelling. He stopped! Suddenly there was quiet in the room. He heard and answered me. He said he had just had a heart attack a few weeks before. Even more shocking things were to come. Immediately after he had spoken, his opponent said that he had lethally high blood pressure and was afraid of death as well.

Words suddenly poured out of me. I knew from experience how painful it is to be a social activist, and how activists often suffer from severe medical problems. I called out, "Be careful, otherwise you will kill yourselves before you can destroy the other." Everyone stopped. Then, those incredible men did something no one could have foreseen.

For some inexplicable reason, the man from the south walked over to the side of the man from the north. Leaving his old role behind, the man from the south put his arm around the narrow shoulders of his opponent. I was stunned. Everyone was stunned. People in the group cried and admired these two men modeling the north and the south coming together just before the actual peace treaty was signed the next evening in Dublin.

I had apparently helped the man from the south to remember his death. In that moment, the man from the north could join him. The topic of discussion had been the killing that had already happened. In a way, death was happening all over again during that discussion. Death was the common denominator, the Dreaming that brought those opponents together.

Those two men reaffirmed my hope in life. They taught me a lot. They showed me that their fury resulted from having seen their own families killed by the opponent. They taught me that death was all around. War is people killing one another. War is Death-Dreaming.

Most of us human beings hate death, we avoid it, forget it, try to overcome it. But death is simply the inevitability of change. Perhaps war is death Dreaming itself into being, trying to make us see it and realize that it is inevitable. Death surrounds us, reminds us that life is short, vulnerable and too valuable to waste.

Nature gives us two choices. We can annihilate one another like that proverbial electron that maintains its stubborn forward movement in time and is annihilated by its opposite. Or we can live the life of a lucid being who, entering a tense field, steps out into eternity. The second possibility in group process amounts to being lucid, getting to the sentient essence of dialogue, noticing what flirts with your attention, getting to the essence of hot spots that flirt with groups. Role switching and Dreaming follow.

Conflict is a master teacher. You learn that you are more than just another person. You and the other merge in a universal principle, the nondualism of Dreaming, the nondualism following the death or relativity of the little you.

How do you maintain 24-Hour Lucid Dreaming awareness during strong group processes? The answer is mindfulness, concentration, and not avoiding events you do not like. Practice. Focus. Train. The world is an awesome meditation hall. Learn to be lucid and conscious while in the midst of it all. I remember Samuel Beckett's advice that was reported to me by one of the conflict participants in Dublin: life is like giving a violin concert while you are learning to play the violin.

 THINGS TO REMEMBER

Have courage and reawaken your community to its lucidity. Share with others the sentient essence of the roles and hot spots that catch your and everyone else's attention.

To change the world, be like the universe, see annihilation coming and switch roles, that is, step out of time and your little self.

Part III. Lucid Living

FOURTEEN

Love Story, the Double

*I Do Not Know Who
Lives Here in my Chest
Or Why the Smile Comes
Am Not myself, more the Bare
Green Knob of a Rose that
Lost every Leaf and Petal to
the Morning Wind.*[89]

**The Rose I Imagine
Rumi Was Talking About**

Who lives in your chest? What is left after all the petals have fallen from the flower? What is left of you after your body falls away?

---

[89] From Barks and Green's, *The Illustrated Rumi*, 97.

Some mystics refer to this essential, eternal you by various names such as the "double." I think of the double as the quality behind all the things that flirt with you. It is the sentient essence, an invisible face behind all other faces, behind the most horrible and magnificent events, the wisdom in your dreams, addictions, and worst compulsions. The double is a part of you that is not human, which relates to and is in constant contact with the rocks, trees, wind, water, earth, the solar system, the whole universe, as well as the ants and elephants and the human realm. The human is just one of many realms.

The double is the Dreaming experience that unfolds into the figures of the Big You. In part two of this book, Lucid Healing, we focused on applying 24-Hour Lucid Dreaming to symptoms, addictions, relationships, and group situations. These applications are like the petals of the flower; they belong to the way your sentient essence manifests in our everyday human life. Now, in this third and final section, I would like to focus on the green knob, the root, the double behind these manifestations. In this chapter, we will focus on direct access to the double. In the final chapters, I will point to the vast implications of 24-Hour Lucid Dreaming for spiritual practice and the future of life on Earth.

THE BIG AND LITTLE YOU

Perennial philosophies and spiritual traditions advise you to identify with what I have been calling the Big You, or the double's nondual world, which exists in everyday life as the elder in you and appears in dreamland as wise figures. A powerful way to learn about the Big You is to remember your death or the death of someone you love. The ancient Chinese sage, Chuang Tsu, put it this way: "The Master came because it was time. He left (died) because he followed the natural flow. Be content with the moment, and be willing to follow the flow; then there will be no room for grief or joy. . . .The wood is consumed but the fire burns on, and we do not know when it will come to an end."[90]

---

[90] *Chuang Tsu*, 59.

In the Taoist way of thinking, the little you is a piece of wood that burns up in time. But the double, here symbolized by the fire, burns on. You will surely die. But the sentient field, the fire or energy of your life, is independent of time and space. You may wonder what this means for your everyday self who worries, tries to live longer, earns money, eats healthy foods and abides by social commitments. From the viewpoint of everyday reality, the fire to which that sage refers is an altered state of consciousness.

As you become more lucid, there are no longer altered states; there is just fire, or flow. The closer you are to living lucidly, the more you appear in the form of the Big You to others. But the sage to which Chuang Tsu refers is not just a grand human figure encompassing all the possible opposites, an elder to those around him. Her own experience is outside the human realm. The sage's human identity has changed; she knows and identifies with the fire of life.

ACCESS TO THE BIG YOU

Do you recall the diagram from chapter 3, which explains the different meanings of lucidity? I repeat that diagram below.

You, IN A DREAM

In the picture on the left, the circle represents a dream in which you are a part. All the other figures are parts of your dream.

THE BIG YOU

In the picture on the right, the circle represents the Big You: that is, You are all the parts of the Dream as well as the sentient feeling in the background.

In the picture on the left, the circle represents a dream in which you are a part. All the bean figures are parts of your dream.

In the picture on the right, the circle represents the Big You: that is, You are all the parts of the Dream as well as the sentient feeling in the background.

The Big You is the source of your dreams; it's another name for the dreammaker. The Big You is the sentient core of everything that catches your attention as well as the things themselves. The double is the Dreaming fire behind the Big You, the fire and intelligence behind your dreams. When you are lucid, you sense the world through the Big You's mind and understand your dreams before you even have them.

The Big You rarely appears as an explicit figure in dreams, because it is all of them, together. Occasionally, the Big You is personified in fantasies as a magnanimous human being, deity, goddess, or god. The Big You might appear as a nature spirit, a wise old woman or man. Some see the Big You as a God or combination of gods. As you work on yourself, the Big You takes on *your face*. At this moment, you are coming closer to your double.

As you grow, the little you becomes more like the whole of you. In your dreams, the little you and Big You begin to look more alike. Thus, even though the double is an invisible, almost unimaginable presence, as you begin to know the Big You and live inside and also outside the world of polarity and duality, the double appears in dreams as your face reflecting that of the Big You.

In your normal state of mind, the little you, bogged down by your concerns about time and people, is out of touch with the Big You. Therefore, this figure appears in a form that is very different from you; it may be a healer or antagonist in dreams, your enemy or ally that must be fought or loved.

The late Carlos Castaneda, an anthropologist who spoke through the voice of his mythic teacher, don Juan, outlined the development leading to the double. During this development, a warrior first wrestles the Big You in the form of a demon who appears as an archenemy.

From the viewpoint of 24-Hour Lucid Dreaming, the Big You first appears in your worst problems, body symptoms, compulsive thoughts, addictions, and relationship and group issues that threaten to overcome you. To succeed in this match, the little you must become a warrior and struggle to interrupt the demonic destructiveness of that formidable inner opponent. As this mythic struggle continues, the successful warrior does not succumb to her apparently insurmountable problems, but survives and finds that her difficulties were but a mask, disguising a power that is now her ally, "the giver of secrets."[91]

By working in the past chapters on your body experiences, symptoms, relationship issues, and addictions, hopefully you too have had the sense that the presence behind your worst problems was that of an uncanny spirit, the Big You. That spirit not only tests the limits of your human abilities but also wishes to join you and extend your identity. Your problems in time and space give it a chance to unfold in the here and now.

In short, your demons become your allies. Through innerwork and meditation, the ally slowly grows to take on your face as you step gingerly out of time and space, growing more like the spirit. In that moment, instead of an ally, you are facing your own Self, and know your double.

An ally waits behind your worst problems, and behind the ally is the Big You and the double, the essence of the changing outer forms including everyone and everything that catches you attention. The Big You or the double is not a spiritual speculation—it appears right now in front of you, in your sentient experience at this very moment. Just look around, pick up what is happening, and there you are, in the core of what you are looking at. In a way, the Big You is trying to flirt with you all the time in the guise of your enemies; it wants to catch your attention and be your love.

To ground the idea of the Big You and the double, you may want to explore the following exercise.

---

[91] See my *Shaman's Body* for more on the ally.

Inner Work—Finding your Double

To do the following exercise, it might be helpful to have a pen and a pad of paper nearby.

To begin with, take a moment and just relax. I want to help you put some of your experiences together. When you are ready, remember some of the exciting and amazing things that have caught your attention in the last few days. Recall the difficult scenes as well. Make a few notes about them. For example, here on the Oregon coast, I remember seeing whales, then there was a terrific fight in one of the neighborhood bars, and a dramatic love scene on TV. Make notes about the things that caught your attention.

Next, try to recall the visions and experiences you had when you first worked on what was flirting with you. Can you remember your divination experience, your sense of time travel, addiction work? Make a note or two about these experiences.

Next, make a few more notes for yourself. What experiences did you have when working on the sentient essence of your symptoms, working with touch, relationships, world issues? We will need these notes in working on the double.

Now let us turn to the present and your imaginations about nature. There are surely several places in the world that you love visiting, or would love to visit if you could. Think now about one of those special places in nature. Think about that part of nature that attracts you the most, perhaps the desert or the high mountains, the seacoast, forest, park, or part of a city. In your imagination, it could be the daytime, or night, perhaps the early morning sunrise. Let your unconscious mind choose the piece of nature that in this moment flirts with you the most.

Now go there in your imagination. Travel to this particular place on Earth and be there at that special time of the day. See it, feel it, listen to the sounds of the Earth there. What do you like so much about this spot? What attracts you about that part of nature? Gaze around slowly and use your lucidity to notice what part of these natural surroundings catches your attention just now. Is this part that catches your attention in front of you, to the right, left, in the back, above, below, or all around you? Look at this part of nature. Study it.

When you are ready, find the essence, the tendency that gave rise to this wonderful piece of nature. Get to its sentient root, its basis. Find its origin, the kind of energy that created it.

Now, shapeshift into being this essence, this nature. What experience of time do you have where you are now? What is space like there? When you are ready, if your mind will allow you, imagine that this part of nature has a mind and eyes of its own. Be this piece of nature; be this mind, see through its eyes.

Take a moment and sketch its eyes, its face, in the space below.

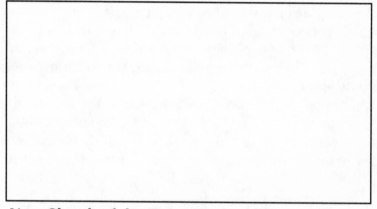

Your Sketch of the Face, Mind and Eyes of Nature

Be this face, this mind, and look through those eyes.

Look at yourself through its eyes. Take a look at yourself. Does nature have advice for you? What message does this viewpoint of nature have for you? Listen to its recommendations. Notice how you look through this viewpoint of nature. Take time with this; the experience may be new and very irrational for your everyday mind. Just trust your creativity, see "its" face, and listen to its message.

If you are your whole Self, it will look and sound like you. If you are closer to your little you, this part of nature will have special, surprising messages. What is the message from nature? How can you use this message in your life both now and in the future? Take the message, the hint, and use it. This may be a lesson you will never hear from a human being. Write it down. Let nature just write about itself; let it speak, if it wants to.

Consider a recent dream as if it were created by this piece of nature. Consider the possibility that this piece of nature is the maker of your dreams. Write down insights about your dream that this piece of nature might give you now.

Finally, ask yourself what part of this grand, Big You has always been familiar to the little you? Can you feel its sentient essence? When you are lucid about this experience, you are close to being your double. Where and when have you felt like the double?

Experiment with feeling this piece of nature within or behind you, working through you. Notice how this feeling influences your relationships with yourself. How does this feeling influence your relationships with others? How could it influence your future? In what manner could this feeling direct you in modifying your relationship to the world? Take a few minutes and ponder these questions about your life.

If you feel like it, take a moment and thank that sentient essence, the part of the Earth where you found your double.

Theory of the Double

I suggest using the part of nature that attracts you the most because the place that attracts you most is the place toward which all the little things that catch your attention converge. Your double is the spirit behind everything that catches the little you's attention. Check this out empirically by looking at the notes you took to answer question number one above, the question about things that have caught your attention recently and experiences you have had while working on yourself over the course of the last few chapters. If you examine those experiences, you may find that the thread connecting them was really the double.

This most attractive thing is a face of the Big You, and its essence is your double. The double is that part of you which is the most wonderful place on earth. You are that hillside, water, or desert. Perhaps that is why Native Americans calls themselves by the names of the Earth near where they were born. They are Low Mountain, Rising Sun, Burnt Hills, White Water, and so forth. You are the Earth.

Let us say you are a person who loves trees. From the viewpoint of consensus reality (CR), the tree is attracting you because you are projecting something onto it; you are discovering the quality of the tree somewhere within your own behavior. In this thinking, there is a separation between the outer and inner tree. You are "projecting," or dreaming it up. This is consensus reality psychology, which can be helpful in understanding yourself.

You   Tree

In CR Psychology, you project something onto the tree

However, from another, more lucid viewpoint, you and the tree flirt with one another and co-arise as aspects of one field. If you drop the viewpoint of parts and follow your Aboriginal sisters and brothers, you and the tree become linked through the experience of Dreaming. There is just "tree-ness" happening. From the sentient viewpoint, you and the tree are one. It manifests through you and you are manifesting through it. In the next picture, I have tried to sketch the new you, as the tree.

Your New Picture

If your view of the most magnificent place in nature never changed, the face you drew of nature would be the face of the Big You. This is as close as we can get in the moment to finding out what You really look like. To be more accurate still, you must be lucid about the sentient essence behind that figure and experience its Dreaming.

The concept of being born with a name in a specific time is a consensus reality way of looking at your life. However, from the viewpoint of lucidity and sentient reality, You were always here, You were never born, and You will never die. In a way, the little you was just one of the petals of your flower. The little you may have always sensed its position relative to the Big You, but because of attachment to everyday reality (and its need for you to be only the little you), you never admit that position or stand for it strongly enough. Perhaps that is why you sometimes fear your death. In a consensus reality sense, "you" lived, but from the viewpoint of 24-Hour Lucid Dreaming, You always were!

GRANDMA

Amy told me a funny story about her grandmother that illustrates these paradoxical ideas. When Amy's grandmother was ninety-seven, she woke up one morning, went to the door to meet a visitor, and quietly asked him if he had seen the newspaper. When the visitor said he had not seen the paper, Amy's grandmother laughed. She replied, "You must read the paper because there, in the obituary column, you will see that I died!"

Dumbfounded, the visitor called Amy and told her this story.

Now, Amy's grandmother was not an ostensible mystic. She worked hard all her life. After retiring, she focused on enjoying herself and apparently loved gambling casinos more than meditation. It was her natural process to simply enter into her double, the Big You, and see through its eyes the demise of the little you. Amy's grandmother was ninety-seven when she realized this; near death, everyone becomes their double, regardless of whether or not they have been working on themselves. Each of us will experience our double; this experience is your natural birthright.

 ## THINGS TO REMEMBER

Wrestle with your worst problems and lucidly explore their essence in order to make them your allies.

As you identify with that essence, you begin to look like your Dreaming. At this point, you develop your double.

To find the immortal double, travel to the most wonderful spot on earth, find and become its sentient essence. Whether we work at this or not, each of us becomes the double.

FIFTEEN

Panacea for the Tragedy of Being a Person

In this very body, six feet in length, with its sense-impressions and its thoughts and ideas, are the world, the origin of the world, and likewise, the Way that leads to the ceasing thereof.
—Buddha

Perennial teachings arise when you realize the limitations of your normal awareness, when you are faced with the infinite, with intractable problems, or when you can no longer find satisfactory explanations for the big questions about life. Gaining access to Dreaming and the figure of the double behind it all is the natural panacea for everyone who has not found answers elsewhere. The double is the answer to the question about why you must die.

In your normal, consensual state of consciousness, you marginalize the sense of the double, and the Big You seems like a horrendous internal group process that has nothing to do with who you are. In this consensual state of consciousness, you are divorced from your double, or from the lucid state's viewpoint; it has agreed to enjoy separating from itself.

Speaking from the state of mind in which the double is reality sounds paradoxical and complex in everyday terms. This is why it is often so difficult to understand ordinary people or spiritual teachers who are lucid about the double. Perhaps only direct experience of the double resolves the confusion about the words used to describe that experience.

Methods for developing a double are basic to perennial teachings. For example, in *Subtle Sound, The Zen Teachings of Maurine Stuart*, Zen master Maurine Stuart echoes perennial teachings: "Enlightenment entails 'seeing clearly.' This doesn't mean that you look at something and analyze it, noting all of its composite parts; no. When you see clearly, when you look at a flower and really see it, the flower sees you."

Her Zen Buddhism is reflected in the theories of the sentient background found in physics and the psychology of perception that we have been exploring in this book. Lucidity is enlightenment for her. In her words, enlightenment means "seeing clearly," looking at a flower in such a way that it sees you.

Stuart goes on, "It's not that the flower has eyes of course. It's that the flower is no longer just a flower, and you are no longer just you. Flower and you are dissolved into something way beyond what we can say, but we can experience this."

Apparently she spoke these lines shortly before she died. I believe that Stuart meant that a sentient attitude involves the dissolution of separateness, the temporary death of the little you, finding the state of consciousness in which you and the flower are one. Reality changes when you are lucid. You and even your enemy are not just friends; you are both different and (even wonderful!) aspects of the same reality that has forgotten itself. Of course, the little you does not find anything wonderful in the opponent, and that too is perfect and as it must be. The Big You is all the parts and the conflict, and the eventual witness, or the Self-seeing itself as that conflict.

Stuart quotes the fourteenth-century German Christian mystic, Meister Eckhart, who speaks about the identity shift that takes place in sentient states. Meister Eckhart's teaching about the union of your soul with God irritated Pope John XXII, who accused the mystic of pantheism, the doctrine that God is the entire universe. Eckhart's thesis was: "The eye with which I see God is the same eye with which God sees me."[92]

This statement soothes something deep inside me that finds it difficult to describe the experience of the double in words. The best way I can explain this experience is to invite you, the reader, on a fantasy trip. If you would like to experiment with the double, see if you can imagine the following. Let us try it together.

Can you imagine standing alone in the mountains or hills early in the morning as the sun is rising? Imagine that wonderful experience. Can you smell the crisp air? You are standing quietly on a mountainside, on a clear morning, enjoying the view of the sun's first rays as they appear from beneath the other mountains between you and the sun. There is only the sound of the wind. You gaze at nature, the mountains, and the increasingly bright light illuminating the darkness of the night.

The Sun

---

[92] This is a quote from Maurine Stuart's excellent, *Subtle Sound* (Boston: Shambhala, 1995). I believe she found this in Meister Eckhart's *Everything as Divine*, trans. Edmund Colledge and Bernard McGinn (New York: Paulist Press, 1996), 20. In that book, he analyzes the act of seeing and speaks of a light which is "uncreated." He says, "In the act of vision, they [the object and viewer, in this case a piece of wood and the human eye] become as one, so that we can truly say that my eye is the wood and the wood is my eye."

Just before sunrise, the upper crest of the mountains in front of you becomes so bright that you feel the sun's light in and around you. This is a soothing, peaceful feeling. Then, as the sun rises, a gradual feeling change takes place inside your heart. You no longer feel like the little you standing and watching, but notice your body straightening up; it lengthens as the sun rises. You rise as it rises. Your body stands straighter than you have ever stood, and as you arise witnessing the sun, you sense the elegance and beauty of that planet as a rising miracle. In this moment, something in you relaxes, and You experience your Self as a planet too, as the sun looking at itself. It is seeing Itself. It knows Its beauty.

You feel like the mirror image of the sun, like the sun itself. Your eyes are its eyes. The eyes with which you are looking at the sun feel to you as if they belong to the sun, now looking back at itself. You see Yourself. And in a way, neither you nor the sun is there any longer. The concepts of the Big You and the double no longer fit; words are concepts, not quite realities. All you can say is that the double knows itself. You experience the universe looking at itself, and the human terms you use to discuss this are interesting but no longer explicit.

Can you follow that fantasy trip? It seems to me that this is what Meister Eckhart meant when he said: "The eye with which I see God is the same eye with which God sees me."

When the double marginalizes itself, when it falls into the pieces and parts and unfolds in the Big You, that is, in your ordinary state of mind, things that are not you seem to flirt with you. In that state of mind, that part of your "eye" that catches flirts from an object is the same eye that the double uses to see you. In mystic terms, God is lucid of Herself. God is the sentient awareness we all share, whether or not we marginalize our lucidity. That eye in me which sees your sentient essence is the same eye in you that sees mine. From the viewpoint of Dreaming, we both use the same eye, the same mind; we are different aspects of the same thing.

Lucid psychology is found not only in mystical Christianity and Zen Buddhism but also in all spiritual or

213

religious thinking. You find it in Aboriginal Africa, Australia; you find it in Islam, in Judaism, in Hinduism. Hinduism uses the path of yoga to gain access to the Big You; Taoism uses Taoist Yoga; Jewish, Christian, and Moslem mystics use prayer, music, and dance.

WAKING UP

You do not need to be a mystic to find God. Everything that happens to you is happening to God. God sleeps and wakes. God argues with Herself; God has financial problems; God is the bank that will not give you the money.

If all this sounds like too much for you, if you have not found Him or Her, wait until tomorrow morning. If you are like most people, you will experience lucidity and the viewpoint of the Big You when you are waking up in the morning. Remember waking up?

Ask yourself, "What wakes you in the morning? Why do you wake up?" When I ask people what wakes them, I received various answers, such as:

- the alarm clock
- readiness to be awake
- my bladder
- my baby
- dreams
- the morning light

- something outside calls you to your attention
- responsibilities in consensus reality
- something inside that tells you to wake up!
- the dog
- God

The next time you are waking up, experiment with maintaining your awareness as you awaken. If you practice lucidity, you will notice that the dreaming process continues as you get up; your mind is dreaming, imagination happens, movements occur. If you are lucid and patiently track sentient experience unfolding into everyday life, you notice that "your" Dreaming awakens you and enters the day because of something you call your bladder, the dog, or the clock.

But then, even after you awaken, Dreaming goes on. It wanders, and if you are wide awake, you might notice that your Dreaming does not quite belong to you; it is nonlocal. Sometimes the Dreaming mind, the Big You, seems to be occurring outside of your body, perhaps above or behind your head. In fact, if you are lucid, you may get the impression that you are the Dreaming witnessing the Dreaming as if it were not you. At the same time, You are the Dreaming happening at some point distant from your body.

Since the Dreaming unfolds itself and appears through the objects that flirt with the little you during the day, you could say that your Dreaming mind is flirting with you, all day long, flirting with itself, trying to awaken you and itself by moving you about, directing you here and there. When She awakens you to Yourself, she is saying, "Awaken and remember me in all that you must see, hear, and feel."

From a larger viewpoint, She is awakening Herself to Herself.

This sounds paradoxical if you are not in a lucid mood. If and when you are, you arrive at the idea that what wakes you up is the Self-reflective process of the universe. She is awakening Herself to Herself. The little you experiences this as being pressed to notice certain things, like your alarm clock, or the dog, your bladder or your body.

In principle, all sentient beings, including the people and the objects you see, are different witnesses and, at the same time, the same witness to the awakening process. You can sense the awakening process happening all day long. All you need to do is recognize Dreaming, pay attention to sentient experience, to the flirts, the mystery of perception, to notice life unfolding, evolving, and creating.

THE COMMUNITY OF ALL BEINGS

The Big You, referred to as Shiva by the Hindus, is a Self-reflection process that manifests everywhere. Everything is Dreaming. Everything is Shiva, including your community's process as well. Let your idea of community expand for a moment so that it consists not only of your friends and acquaintances, but also of all sentient beings, everything that lives, everything you notice. Can you do that for a moment? It may require a shift in your attention, but allow yourself to sense that you are the things you notice, the sentient essence of everything that catches your attention.

If you are close to your Aboriginal background and the Dreaming, you feel your community is the Big You, consisting of all the people in your group, your city plus the buildings, the fish, the sky, the mountains, the water, rocks, and rivers. In other words, everything is You, and the family of the little you.

According to quantum physics and sentient psychology, each of the apparently separate beings you think about are reflecting and sending signals in nonconsensus reality (NCR) to one another. According to the math of quantum mechanics, all these signal exchanges happen at the speed of light (or faster). These infinite sentient interchanges awaken and create what you experience as your little self, your friends, and larger family.

The point is that the consensus (CR) world is far from banal! It is an incredible treasure. Everyday reality is a picture of the universe, awakening in the midst of creation. In other words, whether or not you awaken in the morning is not up to you. You have no choice. You must awaken in the morning in part because the Big You, the larger sentient community, is creating you while It is awakening. The experience of 24-Hour Lucid Dreaming experience gives you personal evidence that your community field unfolds and creates each of its individual parts.

From your normal state of mind, you think you provoke and dream up others, or that they provoke and dream you up to respond the way you do. Everyone thinks they are either the cause or the victim of what is happening around them. But from the perspective of the Dreaming, what is happening between all of us little selves is the community, the Earth manifesting and knowing itself.

From your little you's viewpoint, the parts cause the problems. You spend your life defending yourself and others, standing for something against something else. The little you and the little me, the little fish and the little city, are the cause and the effect of all that happens. All the problems on Earth seem to be caused by the oppressors, the ones who are unconscious, stupid, unknowing.

But from the viewpoint of 24-Hour Lucid Dreaming, of the double, whatever happens occurs because the Big You is unfolding Itself into the world of parts, disentangling Itself, forgetting itself, creating separations, seeing the beauty in each of us as being utterly different, and finally remembering and seeing Itself again as the other.

The little you is a person with your name, the unfolding of a piece of this community. The Big You is the community, made up of you and those oppressive (or wonderful) situations that the little you compulsively focuses on. Your fate is to act out and express the viewpoint of the little you. But the Dreaming that creates you is creating me, and is partially created by me. In other words, your individual feelings and process are mine as well. We are all creating that incredible drama called "Life," which is looking at itself.

When you become lucid, you appreciate and also detach from who you are and have more compassion for me. In fact, you can switch roles because you know you are all the roles.

Thinking in terms of the little you and the Big You makes you careful about using the concept of personal growth or individuation because the individual and personal sense of individuation marginalizes the effect of the community you are living in.

Individuation is a useful term, but it is insufficiently relativistic. The concept of self-development or individuation works best if it is linked to a given consensus reality, since your development depends on the interaction, difference, and similarity between you and your community or world. You do not develop—It develops, just as it is not you who awakens and gets up in the morning, It does this. The little you would never have the ability to awaken, or to have the energy of life. The Big You does all these things.

Likewise, when the little you feels that you are failing at something, it is seeing itself only personally, forgetting itself, marginalizing the winner, which is another part of that community of beings. The little you can neither win nor lose, succeed nor fail, be good nor bad. Those experiences can only happen to the little you relative to the rest of the community of sentient beings; those experiences are aspects of the Big You, competing with and awakening Itself.

This sounds paradoxical only if you see things from the little you's viewpoint of consensus reality. When your everyday mind relaxes for a moment, it will understand. Perhaps this story about the mystic poet Rumi will help the little you understand.

One day in thirteenth-century Turkey, Rumi and his old friend Shams were playing chess. While the two were playing chess, it suddenly became apparent to Rumi that in the next couple of moves, he would lose the game and get checkmated.

"Oh, I've lost," he says in a mock despair.

Shams suddenly looks at him.

"You've won," he says, and their friendship goes to a deeper level of realization.[93]

---

[93] From Coleman Barks and Michael Green, *The Illustrated Rumi* (New York: Broadway Books, Bantam, 1996), 100.

In other words, when you lose, you win, because It is always losing and winning, sleeping and waking up, dying and being reborn, feeling depressed and enthusiastic.

THE BIG YOU IS NOT QUITE HUMAN

You may remember from the sentient dreaming process of the *Abhidhamma*, discussed in chapter 4, that the little you is not needed to experience things in the earliest stages of perception. In fact, the flirts behind observation simply happen; marginalization of these flirts occurs without the little you knowing about it. Remember that there is no "I" involved in the flirt process. According to these ideas, you do not need a human observer for reality to be created. You do not need a "human form"; you only need the idea of sentient beings to create a universe.

Until now most physicists have thought that you needed a conscious observer for the laws of physics to exist, although native peoples said the Dreaming created the universe. But the Dreaming unfolds itself. You do not need a human observer for consciousness to come about! Consciousness is not a first principle; it is generated from a sentient and Dreaming universe. You do not need someone out there to be already present. No human form was necessarily there "in the beginning." Sentient nature, capable of Self-reflection and curiosity, is enough to awaken lucidity. Curiosity and lucidity are first principles, so to speak.

This sounds far out, and it is also basic and fundamental. I think the creator of the black hole theory, physicist John Wheeler, might agree. During his 1979 lecture celebrating Einstein's hundredth birthday, he described a universe as a being with a tail and an eye. The tail represents the early stages of the universe, which are later promoted to concrete reality by means of its own Self-reflection.[94]

---

[94] See my *Quantum Mind*, chapter 36, for more about the Self-reflecting Universe.

The Universe Looking At Itself

Thus the mystical NCR experience of thoughts and consciousness co-arising, and the mathematical structure of quantum physics imply that, as individual people, you and I can relax. From the CR viewpoint you need to develop consciousness, you need to become lucid. But from the viewpoint of the Dreaming, consciousness happens. It simply arises.

The little you and me need to work at consciousness, but You as a whole can relax. The concept of a Self-awakening universe implies that you and I will awaken without doing anything, and that you and I shall remember the Big You. We forget and the world of duality arises, and we remember, and see the Dreaming as the source of reality.

Noticing occurs automatically. Each of us inherits the same spontaneous curious, creative power and wisdom from nature, and each awakens and knows what to do when the time is right. Of course, the everyday you does not trust or believe this. But no matter. That is the Big You again, now forgetting Itself.

You and I often think we are needed to awaken one another and ourselves, and that is true from the little you's viewpoint. But what we call awakening one another is, from the Big You's viewpoint, nature awakening Herself. Awakening happens. It is great to learn the awareness techniques of medicine, psychiatry, psychotherapy, spiritual traditions, and social action. They are especially useful when you are identified with the little you. But they do not solve the bigger problem, the tragic ending of your life.

Let us develop and use these techniques to solve as many problems as possible. But when they no longer work, you automatically fall back to the Dreaming, to sentience, and you experience how lucidity of the Dreaming and consciousness of diversity tend to arise by themselves.

Only when you marginalize sentient experience do you experience yourself as *only* a human being. While from the little you's standpoint, there are many wonderful aspects of being human, and while you as a person may consider yourself to be significant or insignificant, one thing will always remain true from the little you's standpoint. From the viewpoint of consensus time, the fate of human beings is tragic. Everyone who has been born is bound to die. All those you loved will die as well. Though most of us try to avoid this tragic truth by marginalizing the process of death occurring within us, one day it dawns on everyone that life is brief and ends too soon.

Under these circumstances, finding a panacea for this tragedy sounds too good to be true. Nevertheless, it exists. Find the double. It is your personal gateway to the sentient universe. The double is an experience in your own terms of how you are the universe. Behind that picture lies sentient experience. Behind the tree, the flower, the stone, the lake, the wind, is the essence of the Earth. Gaining access to that flower-ness, tree-ness, stone-ness, water-like, wind-like nature transforms you.

Of course, Dreaming is a fate propelling you to evolve your identity as a human being. But Dreaming also asks, even provokes you to explore other identities, including your basic sentient nature. Lucidity teaches you that you are the essence of the things you love most.

If someone says they will miss you when you die, tell them to know themselves, find their double to know who you really are. If you fear you shall miss someone else, know them, find them, search out their most beloved spot, and then you will remember and know Your Self, and the other as well. In each moment that you realize that you are the sentient tendencies behind what attracts you, you celebrate the moment of your own birth. Every day is your birthday, even if you sometimes forget. Happy birthday, every day!

Try the panacea for being human, either now or tomorrow morning when you awaken. Listen with your ears, then get beneath the sound; look with your eyes and reach beyond the outlines of what you see. Feel your feelings, and use sentient attention to lucidly explore the source behind the things that catch your attention. Be that source. Do not just use your ears and eyes, use your lucidity to hear and see Yourself. Get to the emptiness behind the veil of what you notice.

Let me say this again. Find the essence that was there *before* you felt what you are now feeling. Let go of the human form for a moment, let go of this fateful tragedy, and look at yourself through the eyes of nature.

Perhaps you will feel like Rumi. Every time he remembered his whole Self, that Sufi mystic celebrated. He said, "For sixty years I have been forgetful every moment, but not for a second has this flowing toward me stopped or slowed."[95]

 ## THINGS TO REMEMBER

Relax. From the viewpoint of the Dreaming, consciousness happens.

The panacea for living the life of a human being is to listen with your ears, and get beneath the sound. Look with your eyes, and see beyond. Feel your feelings, and lucidly explore the source behind all things catching your attention.

---

[95] Barks and Green, *The Illustrated Rumi*, 107.

SIXTEEN

Diamond Center
of the Mandala

Essence is Emptiness
Everything Else,
Accidental . . .
In This World of Trickery
Emptiness
Is what your Soul wants.[96]

Rumi's "Emptiness" echoes what the Tantric mystics suggested; that only "the universal void exists, everything is not real."[97] In other words, the Tao that cannot be said, the inexpressible, sentient, naked Self, is all there is.

---

[96] Ibid, 104.

[97] According to Buddhist tradition, Tantrism, which focused on sentient experience, first appeared in India under the name of Vajrayana, the Diamond Vehicle. Mircea Eliade, in his detailed work, *Yoga, Immortality and Freedom*, as translated by Willard Trask (Princeton, N.J.: Princeton University Press, 1997), says Tantrism is essentially process; "Among the many meanings of the word Tantra (root *tan*

There are many different names for the Great Spirit of which we are all a part. Tantra had Buddhist, Hindu, and Jainist forms. We saw earlier that in Buddhism, the sentient Self or void was also called the Buddha Mind. In Hinduism, this void was likened to the goddess, Shakti, the feminine cosmic force. She was the power of the "universal void," the divine Mother who sustained not just the real universe and all its beings, but also the many and various manifestation of the gods, the imaginary universe.

She was a figure of the Big You. To use the terms of the present text, Shakti was the primal power of sentient experience, the creativity generating reality. The mystic Tantric practitioners worshipped Shakti by worshiping the whole universe.

Tantra was originally the "religion of the Mother." In earliest times, this religion reigned over the immense Aegeo-Afrasiatic territory. According to Tantrism, all contraries are illusory—extreme evil coincides with extreme good.

Today, we can understand this Tantric teaching from the viewpoint of 24-Hour Lucid Dreaming. From this viewpoint, everything in consensus reality is equally important because it is a manifestation of the whole. Yet, from the viewpoint of the Dreaming Shakti, consensus reality is "maya," or unreal.

According to Tantric traditions, the all-powerful essence connecting to Shakti, the void, the generator of the universe, is symbolized by the diamond. The diamond represents that which is impenetrable, invulnerable, and imperishable in the face of fire and rain, life and death. The diamond with its

---

"extend," "continue," "multiply"), one concerns us particularly—that of "successions," "unfolding," "continuous process."

In A.D. 400-600, Tantrism was a pan-Indian movement that was assimilated by all the great Indian religions and sectarian schools. There were Buddhist, Hindu, Jainist, and other forms of Tantrism. Eliade points out that the idea of the "Great Goddess," the source of reality, acquired a predominant position at that time. (Earlier there was Prajnaparamita, or Supreme Wisdom, and Tara, the great Goddess of ancient India).

perfect crystalline symmetries is a symbol of permanence; clarity, lucidity, hardness, and reflectivity.[98] The diamond's Self-reflective nature is what I have referred to as the double.

This diamond, which symbolizes access to the imperishable part of yourself, was the goal of ancient Tantric mystics. Focusing or worshipping sentient experience creates lucidity, knowledge of Shakti. In short, developing 24-Hour Lucid Dreaming is represented in Tantra as developing a diamond body.

In Buddhist and Tantric thinking, states of unhappiness, suffering, and illusion come from being attached to consensus reality, the world of duality that separates observer and observed. In the Hindu system, Shiva and Shakti, meditation and lucidity, awareness of how the Big You creates the world, marries the observer and the observed. Tantric practitioners saw the world as a symmetrical picture called a "mandala." The practitioner experienced the world arising out its own central point or void, much as physicists today see the universe as arising out of an imaginary realm within the so-called "singularity point" in Einstein's relativity theory.[99]

To reach the experience of the diamond and imperishable body, the Tantric practitioner meditated on the center of the mandala. A typical mandala form is shown below.

Typical Mandala

---

[98] According to Eliade, becoming a diamond was the goal not only of the Buddhist Tantrika but for Indian alchemists as well. The diamond for them was a unity, which contained all else.

[99] See chapter 18 in my *Quantum Mind*.

To give you a sense of how their practice evolved, think of one Tantric teaching that began by imagining that your heart contains a solar mandala resting on a lotus with eight petals. Then, according to ancient practice, you must remember the world is "without a self of its own, without subject, without object, and meditate on emptiness" repeating, "My adamantine essence is knowledge of the void."[100]

The practitioner imagines that the universe radiates from this central sentient essence, found at the center of the mandala. At the same time, this sentient essence was the Buddha radiating out into the world. If you succeed at this viewpoint, you attain the Buddha Mind.

To make the transition from time and space to what I have been calling the heart of lucid dreaming, the adept submerged herself again and again in the central point of the mandala until she reached the state of nonduality. This mystical ritual of entering the central point symbolizes the quiet center at the heart of worldly events, their sentient essence, the Dreaming. This is the most permanent and unchanging place, at "the center of the universe."

The viewpoint of many Hindu and Buddhist teachers (and most mystics) has been that only this central essence of events is real. When you are in a lucid mood, you feel this way too. When you are lucid, you begin to feel that the little you part of your Self should not even ask questions. In fact, the search for answers seems like an unfortunate accident, a tragedy resulting from attachment to CR, a form of addictive behavior, or a forgetfulness that marginalizes the Dreaming.

Nevertheless, with all due respect to the Big You and the Buddha Mind, when you are *not* lucid, the world seems like an impenetrable mystery. You constantly stumble over problems and feel blocked. Desperately, you look to others or to history to find solutions. With luck you find an answer, but then, marginalizing the source from which it came, you

---

[100] Eliade, *Yoga, Immortality and Freedom*, 208.

need another solution each day, and so it goes. But then, the little you is part of the diversity in consensus reality. Against the little you, the larger You appears. Likewise, against the larger You, the "unsolved problems" of the little you can be appreciated. Without darkness, light has no meaning.

It seems to me that IT delights in diversity, in the contrast between parts in everyday reality and between this reality and Dreaming. Because of this multifaceted diversity, It can reflect and see Itself. In any case, you suffer from time, vaguely sensing that you are too locked up in time. This mood drives you to learn some practice, to pick up some kind of meditation, to become lucid again.

Identifying with the center of the mandala, the diamond of lucid Dreaming, is vastly different from the unstable path of identifying with its manifestations, the petals and events of everyday life. The state of the Buddha Mind, the Big You, feels sustainable and imperishable when you are in it. It is a path of lucidity, of insight into the nature of the co-arising of all events. This state is beyond the uncertain world of questions and CR solutions.

When you are lucid, you realize that no single answer is going to help. Or rather, there is only one answer to all questions, which involves staying with the cloudedness of your ordinary senses, close to that which cannot be said, the unspeakable at the center of reality.

LEGAL TROUBLE

As I have implied, the diamond point becomes important when you are troubled and dissociated from the Big You, as I was recently when I ran into legal trouble. I tell this story now because it is one small example of my attempt to practice 24-Hour Lucid Dreaming in the everyday world of space, time, and conflict.

My story begins some years back when Amy and I worked for a Native North American group. At a later point, our freely given work was generously rewarded when native people in another section of the United States heard about our work. They decided to allow us to build on what had previously been Native American property.

Together, with the help of distant neighbors in those wonderful mountains, we dug a common well for water. The neighbors disagreed on what they owed for the well, and Amy and I were pressed to enter into legal proceedings to get back what we were due. The neighbors insisted on their side of the story, while we took our own side.

This was the first time in my life I had to use legal means to solve a business problem. The little me thought, "The legal system was against my moral principles." Why did I have to be involved in all this? The little me thought the legal problems were not worth my time. Who me? Need the court system? Never! After all, I was supposed to be an experienced conflict resolution practitioner!

Why should I have to go to court? Why did I need all this now, as I was finishing this book? Indeed, I needed it. I took the following notes on my fearful state of mind that occurred the night before the trial, the day before completing this book.

"Last night I slept only fitfully. I was miserable, tossed and turned in bed, afraid, and could not understand why. Everything felt too irrational. I could not work on myself. I went to bed, feeling like a mess, hoping something would help."

Amy and I fell asleep. In the middle of the night, Amy rolled over and her hand took mine, waking us both. In the darkness and in my groggy state, I asked her why she had awakened me. She let out a small groan, mumbled that she did not know what was happening, and rolled over. We both fell asleep again.

The next morning, as I was awakening, I realized that Amy's hand was from the Big Amy. The little me needed to wake up in the night and see the legal system as part of the Big Me, not only as different from me. I was suffering from a lack of lucidity, from experiencing my opponent as differ-ent than myself!

After getting up that morning, I sat quietly for some time, staring out the window into the mountains. Something changed in me. I wrote, "I am not me, but the legal system and myself and my opponents, all together. The legal system insists on the CR laws, though the little me hates rules. Thank God for that neighbor. Ah ha! Now I remember. I am the opposing neighbor who brought all this into consciousness. I am the little me who thought he was better than the neighbor and the court system."

Shocked by my observations, I went on. "The little me needs the Big Me to wake up. The Big Me is using the little one's suffering to rediscover Itself. Ha! I guess I wrote this book to remind myself of these things. I am the teacher and the learner, the author and the reader, myself and the opponent." As soon as I felt this, I fell into a state of peacefulness.

When you are close to it, the diamond of lucid dreaming is a pleasure. Even before you must appear in court, even before you must be cross-examined for the first time in your life, all events have already occurred. You are the atmosphere of tension and its creator. The diamond of lucidity, 24-Hour Lucid Dreaming, tells you that this tense atmosphere is perfect; It created conflict. It created that court system, the neighbor, the author, the reader, and the fearful and angry me. All of this gives me the chance to serve the Big You, getting a glimpse into its awesome presence.

My report went on. "I was relieved from my compulsive fears, felt detached, got dressed, and drove to court. While cruising on that backcountry road, just minutes before arriving at the courthouse, I found myself entranced by the beautiful mountain scenery. I felt strangely well. In that state, everything was fine. Whatever occurred would be fine as well. I looked forward to what would happen; I was no longer attached to winning or losing. I had an uncanny feeling that I had already won something I could never lose, and lost something—the little me—I might never regain."

I remember thinking to myself, Ah ha! Perhaps this is what that monk experienced while the tiger was chasing him. (See page 42.) He got to the edge of the cliff, jumped, caught onto a twig, and then saw and admired that strawberry. I laughed and laughed when I first wrote that story.

Only now did I fully realize that story was mine as well. In any case, I found the next sentence in my notes, "While I detest the scene I must enter, simultaneously, I feel it is right." I awakened for that moment and loved the entire mess. Life could not have been more perfect!

What a true pleasure to have the chance to be lucid and conscious. The Big Me knew that for me and each of us, the mess you get into is right in some way, even if it is a court trial. Again and again, realizing this is always realizing it for the very first time.

If you are in trouble, consciously try to examine the problem. First fight the mess, resist it, and try to do away with it. Then, notice the impossible field from which your problems arise, get to the center of the mandala. Experiment with feeling that field; become its various parts, feel what is happening. See yourself and the others on a stage in a grand play. Notice what you have done to the other and what they have done to you. Do what you must, and see the other doing what he or she must as well. Can you see yourself and all the others as spokes of the great mandala?

This reminds me of the great Irish playwright, Oscar Wilde. When accused of being gay and questioned in court about his relationships, when faced with his earlier lovers who had turned against him (after they were paid to do so), he said, "Their poison is part of their perfection."

Today I understand his statement. Everyone, even the one you detest the most, is perfect in the sense of sentient experience, in the sense of being part of the Big You, awakening again to itself. When you are lucid, you have compassion not only for your own behavior, but also for the one who betrayed you. After all, you are "the other" as much as you are not the other.

The diamond of lucid dreaming means being at the center of the story you are in, lucid of the field and conscious of its parts. If you are ill, try to find a cure. If your body is still in pain, do not just solve or resolve the pain. Stay close instead to the sensation behind that symptom. If you have a question about an exam, a job, about a relationship, try to find answers. But remain close to the sentient essence that was there before you even defined the problem you were pondering.

Getting answers to questions is a necessary but unstable path of happiness and misery. It is human, but less sustainable than getting to the sentient essence by knowing all the parts, being them, and creating them. If you can remain in contact with the sentient essence while you go through your everyday life, then you know who You are. From the viewpoint of Dreaming, you can only be what you were before birth and after death, a sentient being, sometimes lucid, always curious, forgetting Yourself and reawakening.

 THINGS TO REMEMBER

Practice identifying with the center of the mandala, the diamond of lucid dreaming, as well as with its manifestations, the petals and events of everyday life.

You can only be what you were before birth and after death, a sentient being, sometimes lucid, always curious, forgetting Yourself and reawakening.

SEVENTEEN

Reality as a Magic Symbol

*When there is no more separation between "this" and
"that," it is called the still-point of Tao. At the still-point
in the center of the circle, one can see the infinite in all
things. Right is infinite; wrong is also infinite.* [101]

This quote sounds like Hindu or Buddhist wisdom, but it is
the old Taoist, Chuang Tsu, telling us that the outcome of
things, right or wrong, is always infinite and somehow right
from the central point, the sentient viewpoint. I guess he would
not have to remind us of this if there was not another process,
which insists that right is better than wrong, winning better
than losing. The most all-embracing state of awareness would
accept, even love everyday reality. It would not inhibit the
inevitable tendency to try and win, and finally, when you start
to lose, it would not inhibit the tendency to burst out laughing.

There is a Zen story about a man on a horse, galloping
along, looking like he is headed for an important place.
Another man, standing on the ground, asks him where he is
going. That is the story.

---

[101] *Chuang Tsu*, 29.

I always imagine weird angles to these wonderful Zen stories. In my mind, the sentient essence behind the story is the relationship between the man on that galloping horse and a man standing quietly on the ground. I see the man suddenly jump into the air with excitement, yelling to the man on the horse to get off because he realizes that he has marginalized his everyday, rushing Self. In this angle of the story, the man on the horse bursts out crying when he sees him jumping on the ground, for he discovers that he is really standing still. Speeding maniacally and standing still, both at the same time are part of the big picture.

To use Taoist terms, the horse is infinite, the rider is infinite, the man on the ground is infinite. The message may be: unconsciously ride that horse—discover centeredness in the race.

All this is easier to say than it is to do. You may remember how I finally appeared in court the day I completed this book. Even though I was fairly centered at the beginning, the court scene lasted seven grim hours and shook me out of my center. The opposing parties and their lawyer entered the room where the deposition was to be held, looking at me as if they were attending a hanging. In typical courtroom manner, the opposing lawyer fulfilled the job he had been trained for and questioned me relentlessly. When I began to answer in my usual combination of facts and feelings, he snapped, "Answer only with a *yes* or a *no*."

I replied that my own lawyer had already told me the same thing; answer only with yes and no. Why, I asked myself out loud, could I not follow their suggestion and answer in terms of yes and no? In spite of the tension I was feeling standing in front of the cameras and jury, my eyes burned so much I had to close them for a moment. In that lucky inner moment, a flickering memory occurred to me. A flirt!

The oath I had taken when I took the stand came floating back into my memory. The court recorder asked me to raise my right hand and repeat after him: "Do you promise to tell the whole truth and nothing but the truth, so help you God?" I remembered solemnly responding, "I do."

Now sweating, facing that dynamic opposing lawyer, this oath came rushing back to me like a flash out of the blue. When he repeated his demand that I answer with "Only yes or no," I responded that I was under oath to tell the "whole truth and nothing but the truth." I apologized to him, saying that the "yes-and-no" answers he demanded of me were not the whole truth. I explained that the whole truth might be inappropriate in his mind, but was nevertheless the whole truth.

So he let me speak about what was on my mind, and I told the whole truth, which included many thoughts, facts, and also feelings. It was an awesome experience. I remember speaking slowly and clearly, enunciating that he was trying to make me look like a criminal, and that it was his job to do so. I actually felt that he was doing his job remarkably well. In my heart, I even admired him. I said that his clients should praise him for his excellent work. If I had wanted someone to take my side, I thought he would have been just the lawyer to get. But I heard myself also saying that in my opinion, he had read too many detective mysteries.

At this point, I noticed that I felt I was winning. I was getting proud of myself; my heart was speeding up and I felt I was getting on my horse. I was galloping. Then something changed in my heart and humility returned, at least for the moment. I heard myself say and that I was interested not just in my own well-being, but also in his well-being and in the future friendship with my opponents. And I meant it.

To make the story short, the opposing party and their lawyer decided to drop the court case and proceed immediately to a settlement. For some reason, the opposing lawyer seemed to me to switch sides, taking my side.[102] At the end of the court proceeding, the opposing party and their lawyer, together with Amy and me, all joined hands. We

---

[102] In fact, this amazing man gave me a ring many months later after all the proceedings had been finished, asking to study with Amy and me. In this way, he and his clients gave me an unforgettable gift.

spontaneously embraced one another. This was not just Dreaming. It was reality. A sense of community occurred. Even before the final settlement occurred, everyone won. As far as the little me is concerned, for that moment in time, I rediscovered the heart of lucid Dreaming.

Now, as I am completing this book, once again I feel like I am on trial with you, this time with myself and also with you, dear reader. Something is asking me to tell the whole truth about dreaming. There is you, our world, and me, all in a courtroom. Something poses the question, who are you? The "yes-and-no answer" to reality is that you and I are people. We come from the same or different nationalities, age groups, genders, sexual orientations, religions, mental and physical health, and so forth. One truth is that there are oppressors and oppressed in the world.

But this is not the whole truth. These are just the yes-and-no answers, the ones that fit our legal systems and political realities worldwide. The whole truth includes the viewpoint of Aboriginal Australians, Zen Buddhists, and native peoples everywhere. That whole truth includes the Dreaming that created each of us.

Knowing about the Dreaming has political consequences. Access to the dark side of the moon has led some Aboriginal Australians to say that you cannot kill the kangaroo, that is only the light side of the moon. The real kangaroo is not its body; the real kangaroo is Kangaroo Dreaming. Being lucid means that everything that is or was real in the consensual sense, is originally a mixture of real and imaginary. It is eternal.

That kangaroo was a song before it took on a body, and Kangaroo Dreaming is free, everywhere, always. You cannot kill it. The body that was shot was a puppet. The dead kangaroo is not the Kangaroo Dreaming, but a momentary figment of the world's imagination.

From the viewpoint of consensus reality, the yes-and-no truth is that you can kill that kangaroo and that you too shall die. But the whole truth is that You are a proud essence, an incredible Dreaming that gives rise to people like your little self and the beings around you. You cannot die because You were never born. In a way, You cannot be buried; no One can be buried. No One ever died.

The truth in terms of "yes-and-no" is that we are individuals. We must stop self-hurt and oppressing others; we need to discover the abuser and the abused, the oppressor and the oppressed and stop the overt annihilation we do through unconsciousness of diversity. We need to clearly see the subtle and manifest hurt, the distance between us, and find out how we marginalize and torture one another, turning history into a blood bath. We need to get on that horse and go faster to see that the mainstream everywhere eradicates minorities, taking their faith and languages and leaving them injured, toppling into their graves.

That is consciousness. The yes-and-no truth is that the oppressors did it. But the whole truth is that You and I did it too. And it was also You and I who fell backwards into the grave after being shot. According to nonlocality and mysticism, "What goes around, comes around." You get what you give.

The whole truth includes the Dreaming, the fact that you cannot kill a person from a nonmainstream group, you cannot submerge a culture—it is always there. You and I are not just individuals. We are a human Earth community, dreaming. We are that culture, dying and not dying, Dreaming. Like the cement buildings above Victoria square in Adelaide Australia, our bodies came some time ago and will eventually fade, but the Dreaming from which that square came, the Dreaming from which we all emerge, will always be.

The yes-and-no truth is that persecution of "minorities" occurs daily. The whole and politically incorrect truth is that even if you stopped persecuting the other, even if you supported political diversity, *if you are not lucid*, you will still perpetrate the ugliest racism against Dreamtime and Your Self and others who are Dreaming. Every time you insist that there is only one reality, focusing only on how we are separate, you commit a crime against the Dreaming.

The whole and most politically incorrect truth is that everything that catches your attention is You. Prove it again for yourself. Take a good look at your Self. Take a few minutes and write down some of the many things that have flirted with you in recent hours. Remember the different objects, the people, the stars at night, the noise on the street that caught your attention.

Now explore those flirts. How are they connected? What is the design behind all those dots, those flirts? The picture unfolding behind and within each thing that catches your attention is your double, a picture of the Big You. Begin connecting the dots, the different flirt-moments, and there You are!

**There You Are
Behind the Dots**

Everything you notice is a point in the outline of the Big You; those gigantic events that bolt out of the darkness of the night, awakening you to their presence, and the tiny things that twinkle, flickering only briefly in front of your attention before they are forgotten. Seeing your whole Self is fun; it is almost child's play.

If you marginalize sentient experience, you think of yourself as a normal human being. If you do not marginalize, others may call you a mystic. Both the everyday person and the mystic are Your faces. Everywhere you look is You, spread throughout time and space. If you do not marginalize sentient experience, you see the face of God even when you look in the mirror.

For the little you, this is true only for moments. The universe seems so alive and constantly changing, making the little you and me so afraid. In normal states of mind, you and I fear this universe and strive to protect ourselves from its awesome power. You and I hang onto our names and refuse to know that the people and events that upset us are the face in the mirror.

EXPLORING THE DARK SIDE OF THE MOON

Using lucidity to explore the dark side of the moon reveals an incredible vision: all the people you hated and loved, who live and who have died, are You. It reveals that you can only say goodbye to someone whose essence you have marginalized.

The truth is that no relationship issue, whether it is about hatred or love, life or death, can ever be completely resolved without lucidity of sentient experience, without 24-hour lucid Dreaming. When you are lucid, you know that you are on both sides, all sides, of relationships.

When you are lucid for (at least a moment), you can delight in the Dreaming, the source of reality. And you also delight in that horrible and spectacular diversity, that reality of contrasts called this world.

 ## THINGS TO REMEMBER

To know your Self, gallop and find yourself standing perfectly still.

Delight in sentient experience and bless the one who marginalizes It.

Forget and remember; You are the bright and dark sides of the moon, the tree and the wind, the coin and the unknown flipping it.

Bibliography

Barks, Coleman, and Michael Green. *The Illuminated Rumi.* New York: Broadway Books, Bantam. 1996.

Bhikkhu, Thanissaro. *Unentangled Knowing: The Teaching of a Thai Buddhist Lay Woman.* Barre, MA: Dhamma Dana Publications. 1995.

Bulkeley, Kelly. *Among All These Dreamers.* Albany, N.Y.: State University of New York Press. 1996.

Castaneda, Carlos. *Journey to Ixtlan: The Lessons of Don Juan.* New York: Simon and Shuster. 1972.

Chuang Tsu. Translated by Gia-Fue Feng and Jane English. New York: Vintage Books. 1974.

Coxhead, David, and Susan Hiller. *Dreams, Visions of the Night.* London: Thames and Hudson. 1975.

Dalai Lama. *Sleeping, Dreaming, and Dying.* Boston: Wisdom Publications. 1997.

Eckhart, Meister. *Everything as Divine: The Wisdom of Meister Eckhart.* Translated by Edmund Colledge and Bernard McGinn. New York: Paulist Press. 1996.

Eliade, Mircea. *Yoga, Immortality and Freedom.* Translated by Willard Trask. Bollingen Series LVI. Princeton, N.J.: Princeton University Press. 1969.

Evans-Wentz, W. Y. *Tibetan Yoga and Secret Doctrines.* New York: Oxford University Press. 1958.

Freud, Sigmund. *The Interpretation of Dreams.* New York: Basic Books. 1953.

Garfield, Patricia. *The Dream Messenger: How Dreams of the Departed Bring Healing Gifts.* New York: Simon and Schuster. 1997.

———. *The Healing Power of Dreams.* New York: Simon and Schuster. 1991.

Goodbread, Joseph. *Radical Intercourse.* Portland, Oreg.: Lao Tsu Press. 1997.

Govinda, A. B. *The Psychological Attitude of Early Buddhist Philosophy.* Delhi: Nag Publishers. 1975.

Griffiths, P. J. *Being Mindless; Buddhist Meditation and the Mind-Body Problem.* La Salle, Ill.: Open Court. 1986.

Guenther, H. V. *Tibetan Buddhism in Western Perspective: Collected Articles of Herbert V. Guenther.* Delhi: Dharma Publishing. 1989.

Hanh, Thich Naht. *The Heart of the Buddha's Teachings: Transforming Suffering into Peace, Joy, and Liberation: The Four Noble Truths, The Noble Eight Fold Path, and Other Basic Buddhist Teachings*. Berkeley, Calif.: Parallax Press. 1998.

―――. *Please Call Me by My True Names*. Berkeley, Calif.: Parallax Press. 1993.

Hilevi, ben Shimon. *Kabbalah, Tradition of Hidden Knowledge*. London: Thames and Hudson. 1979.

Jung, Carl. *The Collected Works*. 2d ed., vol. 8. *The Structure and Dynamics of the Psyche*. Princeton N.J.: Princeton University Press. 1969.

―――. *The Collected Works*. vol. 14. *Psychology and Alchemy*. Princeton N.J.: Princeton University Press. 1970.

Kaplan-Williams, Stephen. *Exploring the World of Lucid Dreaming*. New York: Ballantine. 1992.

Krippner, Stanley, and Joseph Dillard. *Dreamworking: How to Use Your Dreams for Creative Problem Solving*. New York: Bearly Limited. 1988.

La Berge, Stephen. *Lucid Dreaming: The Power of Being Awake and Aware in Your Dreams*. New York: Jeremy Tarcher. 1985.

Lancaster, B. L. "The Mythology of Anata." In *The Authenticity Of Experience*, edited by J. Pickering. Richmond, Surrey, UK: Curzon Press. 1998.

————. "The Stages of Perception: Towards a Synthesis of Cognitive Neuroscience and the Buddhist *Abhidhamma* Tradition." *Journal of Consciousness Studies,* 4, no. 2, (1997).

Lao Tzu. *Tao Te Ching: The Book of Meaning and Life.* Translation and Commentary by Richard Wilhelm, translated into English by H. G. Ostwald. New York: Arkana-Penguin. 1986.

Lawlor, Robert. *Voice of the First Day, Awakening in the Aboriginal Dreamtime.* Rochester, Vt.: Inner Traditions International. 1991.

Mathews, John, consulting ed. *The World Atlas of Divination.* Boston: Bulfinch Press. 1992.

Mbiti, John. *African Religions and Philosophy.* 2d ed. Reprint. Oxford, UK: Heinemann Publishers. 1997.

Mindell, Amy. *Metaskills, the Spiritual Art of Therapy.* Tempe, Ariz.: New Falcon Press. 1994.

————. *Coma: A Guide for Friends and Helpers.* Portland, Oreg.: Lao Tsu Press. 1999.

Mindell, Arnold. *Dreambody: The Body's Role in Revealing the Self.* Portland, Oreg.: Lao Tsu Press. 1998.

————. *Working with the Dreaming Body.* London: Penguin-Arkana. 1984.

————. *River's Way: The Process Science of the Dreambody.* London: Penguin. 1985.

————. *The Dreambody in Relationships.* New York: Penguin. 1986.

———. *City Shadows, Psychological Interventions in Psychiatry.* New York: Penguin. 1987.

———. *Coma, Key to Awakening, Working with the Dreambody near Death.* New York: Shambhala/Penguin-Arkana. 1988.

———. *Inner Dreambodywork: Working on Yourself Alone.* New York: Penguin. 1989.

———. *The Year I: Global Process Work with Planetary Tensions.* New York: Penguin-Arkana. 1990.

———. *The Leader as Martial Artist: An Introduction to Deep Democracy, Techniques and Strategies for Resolving Conflict and Creating Community.* San Francisco: HarperCollins. 1992.

———. *The Shaman's Body: A New Shamanism for Health, Relationships and Community.* San Francisco: HarperCollins. 1994.

———. *Sitting in the Fire: Large Group Transformation through Diversity and Conflict.* Portland, Oreg.: Lao Tse Press. 1995.

———. *Quantum Mind: The Edge between Physics and Psychology.* Portland, Oreg.: Lao Tsu Press. 1999.

———, with Amy Mindell. *Riding the Horse Backwards: Process Work in Theory and Practice.* New York: Penguin. 1992.

Monroe, Robert. *Journey out of the Body: Ultimate Journey.* New York: Doubleday. 1994.

Moss, Robert. *Conscious Dreaming.* New York. Crown Trade Paperback. 1996.

Norbus, Namkai. *Dream Yoga and the Practice of Natural Light.* Ithaca, N.Y.: Snow Lion. 1992.

Perls, Fritz. *Gestalt Therapy Verbatim.* Moab, Utah: Real People Press. 1969.

Raheem, Aminah. *Process Acupressure.* Palm Beach Gardens, Fla.: Upledger Institute. 1996.

Rawson, Philip, and Laszlo Legaza. *Tao, the Chinese Philosophy of Time and Change.* London: Thames and Hudson. 1979

Reed, Henry. *Awakening Your Psychic Powers.* New York: St. Martin's Press. 1996.

Rumi. *The Essential Rumi.* Edited, trans. by Coleman Barks. San Francisco: HarperCollins. 1995.

Rhys-David, C. A. F. *Buddhist Psychology: An Inquiry into the Analysis and Theory of Mind in Pali Literature.* In *Compendium of Philosophy,* S. Z. Aung and C.A.F. Rhys-David. Boston: Wisdom Publications. 1979.

Schwarz, Salome. "Shamanism." Ph.D. Thesis. Union Institute. Yellow Springs, Ohio. 1996.

Shearer, P., trans. *Effortless Being: The Yoga Sutras of Patnajali.* London: Unwin. 1989.

Stuart, Maurine. *Subtle Sound: The Zen Teachings of Maurine Stuart.* Boston: Shambhala. 1996.

Tansley, David V. *Subtle Body: Essence and Shadow.* London: Thames and Hudson. 1992.

Tart, Charles. *Altered States of Consciousness.* New York: John Wiley and Sons, 1969.

Thera, Venerable Nyanaponika. *Abhindhamma Studies, Buddhist Explorations of Consciousness and Time.* Boston: Wisdom Publications. 1998.

The Upanishads: Breath of the Eternal. Translated by Swami Prabhavananda and Frederick Manchester. Hollywood, Calif.: Vedanta Press and Bookshop. 1996.

Von Franz, Marie Louise. *Time, Rhythm, and Repose.* London: Thames and Hudson. 1978.

————. *On Divination and Synchronicity.* Toronto, Canada: Inner City Books. 1980.

Walsh, Roger N. *The Spirit of Shamanism.* New York: Jeremy P. Tarcher/Perigee. 1990.

————. "Lucid Dreaming: Some Transpersonal Implications." *Journal of Transpersonal Psychology* 24, no.2 (1992): 193-200.

Watts, Alan. *The Book: On the Taboo against Knowing Who You Are.* New York: Vintage. 1972.

Williams, Cecil. *No Hiding Place, Empowerment, and Recovery For Our Communities.* San Francisco: Harper. 1994.

Wolf, Fred Alan. *The Dreaming Universe: A Mind-Expanding Journey into the Realm Where Psyche and Physics Meet.* New York: Touchstone. 1995.

Index

the Abhidhamma
  perception in, 50
  teaching of, 45-64
Abhidhamma Studies, 54, 57
Aborigines. *See* Australian
  Aborigines
addictions
  changing the atmosphere that
  creates, 162-172
  community work on, 165-166,
  170
  confronting, 166
  connected with identity, 163-
  164
  medical interventions, 165
  methods of working on, 164-168
  re-accessing, 167-168
  and relationships, 162-172
Adelaide, Australia, 3
alarm clock story, 57-60
Alcoholics Anonymous (AA),
  165
ancestral memory, 116
"A'NE HIMU," 19
angry expression, 133-135
animals
  hearing dream songs, 21
animus and anima, 176-178
answers, 230-231
anthropos myths, 90
archetypes
  Jung's theory of, 10
Aspect, Alan, 175

association
  with dreams, 29
atmosphere, 152
  that creates addictions, changing, 162-172
attachment to everyday reality,
  12
  overcoming, 59, 110
Aurobindo, Sri, 21
Australian Aborigines
  dominated and decimated by
  Europeans, 12-13
  sentient psychology basic to, 73,
  87
  traditions of, viii, 9, 36, 46
awakening. *See also* Waking up
  defining, 14, 22
  example of, 57-60
  happening, 220
awareness, 36
  levels of, 180-181
  training in, 152, 181-182

"backwards in time theory"
  of magnetic field activity, 119-
  120
"bare attention"
  developing in Buddhist
  thought, 34, 57
barriers story, 151-152
beeping diagrams, 79-97
bells chiming, 187-188
Bell's theorem, 174-176
big dreams, 150-152

The Big You, 33, 40-41, 44, 61,
81, 199-209
accessing, 201-203
marginalizing, 182
not quite human, 219-222
unfolding, 200
birds
hearing dream songs, 21
body symptoms
addressing directly, 135
nonlocal origin of, 128-142
Bohm, David, 10, 174
Brahma, 19-20
The Buddha, 45, 57, 210
"Buddha mind," 81-82, 85, 92
Buddhism, 15
Deep Purple, 45-64
Japanese, 39
sentient psychology basic to,
73
stages of perception in, 46-51
Buddhist thought, 36, 64
developing "bare attention" in,
34, 57
foundations of, ix
ideas of perception, 11
"bump theory"
of magnetic field activity, 119-
120

Cabrini, Mother, 107-108
Castaneda, Carlos, 74, 202
Chamberlin, Jim, ix
charged particles, 117
children
reprimanding for being
dreamy, 12
Christianity, 187
Chuang Tsu, 11, 18, 20, 29, 43,
79-80, 82-85, 115, 128, 200
clairvoyance, 107
clamp analogy, 140-141
cleaning example, 70-71
"cleanup clinics," 165

cloudedness, 103, 105, 108
cognitive mind
relaxing, 25
colonialization, 12
the common cold
teaching of the Abhidhamma
and, 45-64
communication
changing your level of, 183
The Community of All Beings,
216-219
community work
on addictions, 165-166, 170
reawakening lucidity in, 196
concentration, 11
conflict
a master teacher, 196
surviving and resolving severe,
186
conflict work
with large groups, 191-193
confronting addictions, 166
Confucius, 45
consciousness, 78
blocking lucidity, 63
cleaning up, 77
defining, 36, 41
meaning and timing of, 210-
222
power to reach, 53
really unconsciousness, 60-64
in therapy, 75-77
consciousness in large groups
lucidity and, 185-196
consensus reality (CR), 15, 20,
42, 46-47, 51-52, 72-73
concepts in, 74
not-doing in, 67
sentient field in back of, 91
cooking, 65-66
countertransference, 145
CR. *See* Consensus reality
Cramer, John G., 86
cramping story, 140-141

da Vinci, Leonardo, 5
Dalai Lama, 19, 22-23
death
  dealing with, 195-196, 221, 235-236
Deep Purple Buddhism, 45-64
déjà vu, 115-116
demons
  making allies of, 202-203
depression, 7, 147-148
detachment, 110
detoxification centers, 165
diamond center of the mandala, 223-231
different realities, 65-78
differentness
  also sameness, 173-184
disenfranchisement, 166
dissociation, 17-29
  from dreaming, 26-27, 29
diversity issues
  working with, 192
divination
  example of, 108-110
  methods of, 103
  patterns of, 101-103
  as process, 107-108
  theory and practice of, 96, 98-110
diviners
  phases of, 102
don Juan, 74, 202
the double, 199-209
  being divorced from, 210
  finding, 204-206, 221
  marginalization of, 213
  theory of, 206-208
double signals, 149-150
"Dream Yoga," 18-19
Dreambody, 14, 129
the dreambody, 129-132
  work methods for, 132-137
dreaminess
  reprimanding children for, 12

Dreaming, 45, 114-115
  with another person, 160, 181-182
  contact with, 171
  as the core energy of life, 7-8
  defining, viii, 17
  dissociation from, 26-27, 29
  divination via, 103
  everyday reality and, 94-95
  gaining access to, 7, 13, 210
  having its own self-protection, 13
  kangaroo, 13, 235
  making sense of, 61
  many names for, 10-13
  marginalizing, 7, 11-12
  mysticism and physics, 3-16
  nondualism of, 196
  political incorrectness of, 232-238
  reality comes from, 15, 20
  recollecting, 25
  seeing amid chaos, 3
  simplifying, 6-8
  24-Hour Lucid, 13-16
  unfolding of, 27, 174
  while awake, 215
  work ethic killing, 12-13
  as worldwork, 185-196
  your experience of, 23-24
Dreaming field, 33
Dreaming reality, 4
Dreaming up, 146-149
dreamland, 15, 20
  at the center *vs.* at the base, 14
  images comprising, 138
  level of reality, 35, 51
dreamlike tendencies, 26
dreams
  associating with, 29
  interpreting, 33
  naturally mysterious, 27
  personal examples, 27-28
dreamtime

the Dreaming, 15, 20
exploring, 11
level of reality, 34-35
and physics, 8-10
power to gain access to, 15-16
dreamwork, 61
lucidity and, 17-29
drives
Freud's concept of, 10
dropping self-definition, 189

East and West, 38
Eastern thinking
foundations of, ix
Eckhart, Meister, 211-213
edges, 54
working with, 150
Egyptian Book of the Dead, 135
Einstein, Albert, 100, 175
electroencephalograms (EEGs),
22
electrons
entering magnetic fields, 117-
125
*Encyclopedia of Eastern
Philosophy and Religion,* 21
energetic tendencies, 11
Enlightenment, 37
defining, 64, 186
East and West, 30-44
multicultural understanding
of, 30-44
spontaneous, 41
symptoms a route to, 142
entanglement
in quantum physics, 160
touch and, 143-161
environmental issues, 193
events
"tangled" with ideas, 72
everyday reality
and Dreaming, 94-95
level of, 35
the nonconsensual realm as

the background of, 173
unfolding of, 10, 19
Western attachment to, 12
existence, 17
experiences
becoming aware of everything
in, 34
of dreaming, 23-24
nontemporal and nonlocal, 71-
75
timeless, 127
unfelt, 134
verbalizable, 24
explosive expression, 133-135
extended self, 182
extending self-definition, 189

fax machine analogy, 87
Feynman, Richard, 116-119,
136, 193
field theory, 176. *See also*
Dreaming field; magnetic field;
relationship fields; sentient field
fish story. *See* Piscean dreaming
"flirting," 54, 56, 68-70, 79-97,
85, 93, 102, 178
appreciating, 181-182
discovering, 159
pattern behind, 237
in reality, 125-127
visual, 175-179
flowers, 140-141, 199, 211
Freud, Sigmund, 28
concept of drives, 10
friendship, 218-219

"getting it," 110
Ghandi, Mahatma, 185
God
playing hide-and-seek with, 89
seeing, 212
Goodbread, Joseph, 147
Grandma's story, 208-209
The Great Awakening, 19

great objects, 55
The Great Realization, 23
"Great Spirit," 11, 224
Great Work, 27
groups. *See* large groups

hands
    sensitizing, 158-159
Hawking, Stephen, 10
the "Healer" and the "Problem"
    nonlocality between, 143-161
healing, 106
    lucid, 113-196
health
    connection with relationships,
    163
Heisenberg, Werner, 8
Heizer, Leslie, viii
Hopi, 19-20

ideas
    "tangled" with events, 72
identity
    connected with addictions, 163-
    164
    your new, 31
"Ignis Innaturalis," 93-96
illness concept, 129, 132
imaginary time, 10
"individuality," 38
individuation, 218
inner work
    finding your double with, 204-
    206
    research on, 24-26
    and world work, 188-189
interconnections, 77-78
Ireland
    working with large groups in,
    194-196
Iroquois, 13

Japanese Buddhism, 39
Johnson, John and Gladys, ix

Joseph, Chief, 12-13
Jung, C. G., 28, 82-85, 99, 176
    theory of archetypes, 10

Kabbalah, 89
kangaroo Dreaming, 13, 235
Kenyan shamans, 73

La Berge, Stephen, 13, 22, 30
Lao Tzu, 26, 94, 98
large groups
    in Ireland, 194-196
    lucidity and consciousness in,
    185-196
    processing the atmosphere in,
    183
legal trouble story, 227-231,
    233-235
level of communication
    changing, 183
levels of awareness, 180-181
levels of reality, 34-35
    dreamland, 35
    dreamtime (or sentient reali-
    ty), 34-35
    everyday reality, 35
life
    creating the incredible drama
    of, 217
The Little You, 40-41, 199-209
    catching the attention of, 206
living
    lucid, 199-238
love
    for yourself, 182-184
lucid dreaming
    defining, 21-22
    diamond of, 229
    exercise in, 138-140
    using to explore sentient reality,
    184
Lucid Dreaming, 13
lucid healing, 113-196
lucid living, 199-238

lucid medicine
  preventive, 128-142
lucid touch
  exercise in, 157-160
lucidity, 217-21878
  blocking consciousness, 63
  and consciousness in large
    groups, 185-196
  defining, 11, 36
  and dreamwork, 17-29
  examples of, 40
  growing in, 15
  increasing, 185
  old *vs.* new meaning, 31-32
  preventive medicine of, 71
  reawakening in communities,
    196
  in therapy, 75-77
lucidity training, 17-29

magnetic field
  theories about, 119-121, 193
the mandala, 225-226
  diamond center of, 223-231
Mandukya Upanisad, 99
marginalization, 33-34, 43, 53-54,
  90-93
  of the Big You, 182
  of the double, 213
  of dreaming, 7, 11-12
  overcoming, 55-57
  of self and others, 38-39
  of sentient experience, 61
Maricopa tribe, 13
Marx, Karl, 185
Matthews, John, 101
Mbiti
  concept of time, ix
  meaning of consciousness, 210-
    222
meaningfulness, 106
medical interventions
  in addictions, 165
medical paradigm, 129, 132

medicine
  lucid preventive, 128-142
medicine people, 73
meditation, 7, 37
  training in, 52, 64
*Memories, Dreams, and
  Reflections,* 82-83
memory
  ancestral, 116
Michelangelo, 5
Mindell, Amy, ix, 3, 55-56, 67-
  68, 140, 208-209, 228
Mindell, Pearl and Carl, ix
mindfulness, 11. *See also*
  "Buddha mind"; cognitive
  mind; subconscious mind;
  unconscious mind
Quantum Mind, 9, 66, 83
moon
  light and dark sides of, 4, 235,
    238
mosquito experience, 53
Mother
  religion of the, 224
movement
  divination via, 103-108
multicultural understanding
  of Enlightenment, 30-44
music
  very close to dreaming, 21
mysticism, 226. *See also* individual mystics and mystic traditions
  putting to work in social
    action, 186-189
mythic viewpoint, 88-90, 92, 152

Nai-mus-ena people, 19
Native Americans, 11-13, 56.
  See also individual tribal
  groups
NCR. *See* non consensus reality
Nez Perce, 12-13
Nibbanna, 54

non consensus reality (NCR),
47, 73
not-doing in, 67
nonconsensual realm, 72
the background of everyday
reality, 173
sentient interaction taking
place in, 154
nonlocal origin
of body symptoms, 128-142
nonlocality
defining, 160
between the "Healer" and the
"Problem," 143-161
nontemporal and nonlocal experiences, 71-75
defining, 72
not-doing, 77
in physics and psychology, 66-
67
of song-writing, 70
of sweeping up, 70-71
not-working on yourself, 65-78
Nyanaponika Thera, the
Venerable, 53, 57, 87

objects and events
power of, 52-55
Obrien, Lewis, viii, 3-5
oppression, 186-187
origin of body symptoms
nonlocal, 128-142
the other
noticing, 189

panacea
for the tragedy of being a person, 210-222
paranoia, 17
partnerships. *See* relationships
party story, 170-172
Patanjali, 99, 107
perception
Dreaming or sentient, 49-51

ideas of in Buddhist thinking, 11
stages of in Buddhism, 46-51
perception in the Abhidhamma
stepwise, 50
photons, 175-177
physics, ix
and beeping diagrams, 79-97
divination via, 103
dreamtime and, 8-10
not-doing in, 66-67
Piscean dreaming, 156-157, 179
plum example, 67-68
political incorrectness
of Dreaming, 232-238
positrons, 118
power
in being a teacher, 148
of objects and events, 52-55,
134
and rank, 145-146
The Powerful Something, 20
preventive medicine
lucid, 128-142
of lucidity, 71
"Primal Force," 11, 18, 20, 29
pristine consciousness, 17-29
Process Work Centers, viii
projection, 85, 144-145
beginning of, 180
psychology, ix, 37-38
and advanced physics, 98-110
and beeping diagrams, 79-97
and divination, 98-110
not-doing in, 66-67
relative youth of Western, 46
visual flirts in, 175-179

quantum physics
sentient psychology basic to,
73, 174
quantum wave potential, 8-9,
16, 102
questions for self-exploration,
24-26

racism, 12, 186-187, 236
Raheem, Aminah, 135
Ramana Maharshi, Sri, 21, 37
rank
  power and, 145-146
rapid eye movements (REMs), 22
re-accessing addictions, 167-168
reality. *See also* different realities; Dreaming reality; everyday reality
  comes from dreaming, 15, 20, 26
  consensus, 15, 20
  flirts in, 125-127
  levels of, 34-35
  as a magic symbol, 232-238
Red Kangaroo Dreaming, 4
Reed, Henry, 99
reflection, 79-97
reincarnation
  and stepping out of time, 113-127
relationship fields
  sentient accessing of, 168
relationship work, 144-153
  methods summary, 153
relationships
  addictions and, 162-172
  awareness exercise for, 181-182
  connection with health, 163
  life-long patterns driving, 151
  unbroken wholeness in, 173-184
research inner work, 24-26
"retroflection," 122
Ricklin, Franz, 124-125
Rinzai Zen, 39
Rumi, Jelaluddin, 143, 173, 218-219, 222
  "emptiness" of, 223

sahaja samadhi, 21, 37
samadhi, 21, 37
sameness
  also differentness, 173-184
  simultaneously discovering, 183

secrets
  holding of, 166
self
  extended, 182
  knowing your whole, 75
self-criticism, 55
self-definition
  dropping and extending, 189
self-exploration
  questions for, 24-26
self-protection
  dreaming having its own, 13
self-reflection, 102, 114, 219, 225
sensitizing your hands, 158-159
sentience
  divination via, 103
sentient addiction work, 168-170
sentient awareness, 38
sentient body work, 135-137
sentient entanglement, 152
sentient experiences, 83, 154-155
  marginalization of, 61
sentient field
  in back of consensus reality, 91
sentient healing
  examples of, 65-78
sentient interactions, 154-155
sentient nature, 219
sentient perception, 49-51
sentient reality, 7, 20
  defining, 36
  level of, 34-35
  using lucid dreaming to explore, 184
sentient realm
  simultaneous lucidity of, 63
sentient symptom exercise, 137-140
sentient touch
  exercise in, 157-160
Shakti, 224-225
shamanism
  sentient psychology basic to, 73

shamans, 73, 101
shapeshifting, 95, 104, 106
  experimenting with, 126, 181-182
Shiva, 216
signal exchange, 149-150
Sleeping, Dreaming and Dying, 18-19
slight objects, 54
small self. *See* The Little You
social action
  pain of, 195
  putting mysticism to work in, 186-189
song-writing
  not-doing of, 70
space ship analogy, 116
"space-time diagrams," 119-121
  understanding, 121-125
spiritual traditions, 7
Steiner, Rudolf, 22
stepwise perception
  in the Abhidhamma, 50
still-point
  of the Tao, 232
"stoned" sensation, 28
Stuart, Maurine, 211
subconscious mind, 6
Subtle Sound, 211
suppressing events, 55
suppression, 55
sweeping up
  not-doing of, 70-71
symptoms. *See also* sentient symptom exercise
  medical, 129-132
  multidimensional manifestation of, 134

Tantric Buddhism, 11, 223-226
The Tao, 11, 17, 29, 45-46, 102, 201
  divination via, 103
  still-point of, 232

that cannot be spoken, 18, 20, 24, 30, 223
Tao Te Ching, 94
Tarnda Munaintya, 4
Tart, Charles, 99
tea ceremony, 75, 78
teaching of the Abhidhamma
  and the common cold, 45-64
teapot story, 80-81
telekinesis, 67
telepathy, 107
tendencies, 9, 16
  discovering, 159, 169
  divination via, 103
  dreamlike, 26
  energetic, 11
therapy
  consciousness and lucidity in, 75-77
Thich Naht Hahn, 36
things to remember, 29, 43-44, 64, 78, 96-97, 108, 127, 142, 160-161, 172, 184, 196, 209, 222, 231, 238
thought
  Buddhist, 36, 64
  understanding, 68-69
tiger story, 41-43
time
  imaginary, 10
  Mbiti concept of, ix
  sequence of events, 71
  stepping out of, 113-127
time travel, 113-127
  exercise in, 125
timeless experiences, 127
timing
  of consciousness, 210-222
touch
  and entanglement, 143-161
training
  in awareness, 152, 181-182
  in lucidity, 17-29
  in meditation, 52

transference
  working on, 144-145
transformation
  the basis of Taoism, 98
transitioning
  between realms, 86-88
24-Hour Lucid Dreaming, 3-16
  example of, 32-34
twisted arm story, 155-156

Uncle Lewis. *See* Obrien, Lewis
unconscious mind, 6
  Erickson's view of, 10-11
unfolding
  of Dreaming, 27, 174
  of everyday reality, 10, 19
  experiment in, 93-96
unintended signals, 149-150

Vassiliou, Lily, viii
verbalizable experience, 24
Victoria Square, 3-4
virtual particles, 110, 117-118, 127
"void," 11

waking up, 214-216
war
  as death-Dreaming, 195-196
Watts, Alan, 89-90
the wheel
  getting off, 110

Wheeler, John, 219
wholeness
  unbroken in relationships, 10,
  173-184
Wilde, Oscar, 230
Williams, Cecil, 165
winning and losing, 218-219
Wolf, Fred Alan, 9
work ethic
  killing Dreaming, 12-13
working on yourself, 168-169.
  See also not-working on yourself
working sentiently
  with others, 159-160
The World Atlas of Divination,
  101
world work
  dreaming in, 185-196
  elements of, 192
  inner work and, 188-189
Worsley, Alan, 22

yes-and-no truth, 236
your new identity, 31

Zen Buddhism, 44, 211
  Rinzai sect, 39
Zen tiger, 41-43